I0835145

THE ANATOMY OF A
CHANGE LEADER

THE ANATOMY OF A

CHANGE LEADER

How to THINK, ACT, and LEAD Change in a Disruptive World

Yvonne Ruke Akpoveta
MBA, C.Dir.

OliveBlue Incorporated

The Anatomy of a Change Leader

How to Think, Act, and Lead Change in a Disruptive World

Published in Canada by OliveBlue Incorporated

www.thechangeleadership.com

ISBN 978-0-9939023-7-6

First published 2026

Cataloguing in Publication data available from Library and Archives Canada

For every change leader who has ever stood in a difficult room and chosen to stay.

For those who choose to evolve and never lose themselves in the process.

And for the community that made this work possible.

Content

Acknowledgements

This book exists because of the work, the people, and the community.

A community that began with The Change Leadership Conference, which has always been more than an event. From the very beginning, it has been a gathering place, a room where people who had spent years carrying the invisible weight of this work could finally feel they were not alone. Every practitioner, leader, facilitator, speaker, and change maker who has walked through those doors, taken a seat, asked an honest question, or shared a difficult story has contributed something to what this book became. They may not know it. But I do.

Beyond the Conference, the stories in these pages belong to the work. They have been gathered across more than two decades of working with professionals and organizations navigating and leading change. Every person who trusted me to be present with them through their change journey shaped my understanding of what change leadership truly requires of a human being. I am grateful beyond what any acknowledgement page can hold.

To my family, friends, everyone, and even strangers who supported me along the way, who spoke words of encouragement, sent that one email, or showed up and supported the work, you are the reason this book exists. You showed me that the work was reaching further than I knew.

And to every reader who picks up these pages, welcome. You are already part of what this community is becoming.

Introduction

Why This Book. Why Now. Why You.

Change is no longer episodic. It is the environment.

The organizations, communities, and workplaces we lead have entered a period of continuous disruption. Technologies emerge and become obsolete within the same decade. Teams are distributed across time zones and screens. Geopolitical shifts abound. Economic uncertainty has become a background condition rather than a crisis to be survived and moved past. Artificial intelligence is reshaping what work means and what leaders must become. And through all of it, the one constant is people. People who are navigating uncertainty, processing loss, holding on to what feels familiar, and looking to their leaders for something they cannot always name but recognize immediately when it is present.

> What they are looking for is not a plan. It is a person.

This is a book about that person. About you.

I did not set out to become a change leader. I did not find the role in a job description or choose it from a list of career options. Change leadership found me, gradually and then all at once, in the gap between what organizations intended and what people were experiencing. I saw it in failed projects. In the frustration of teams that were never told why. In the resistance of people who were never asked what they feared. In the fatigue of leaders who were carrying everyone else without anyone carrying them. And I saw, equally, what became possible when someone in the room chose to lead differently regardless of role or title. When a change leader paused before reacting. When they asked a better question. When they stayed present in a moment that everyone else was anxious and uncertain.

I have spent my career in that gap. And everything in this book comes from it.

The Anatomy of a Change Leader is built on a simple but significant premise: that the most powerful thing a change leader brings to any room is not their methodology. It is their anatomy. The way they think. The way they act. The way they lead. The way they are grounded in something deeper than outcomes. The Head, the Heart, the Hands, and the Soul are not competencies to be trained.

They are dimensions of a way of being that develops over time, through experience and reflection and the willingness to stay honest about where you are still growing.

The book is organized around our proprietary Change Leadership DNA framework: Discover, Navigate, Apply.

Discover is where we begin, and where every change leader must begin. Before you can lead others through uncertainty, you need to understand who you are in it. Part I explores the inner work of change leadership through the four dimensions of the anatomy. *The Head*: how you think, make sense of complexity, and bring clarity to people who are disoriented. *The Heart*: how you connect, build trust, and lead with genuine empathy rather than its performance. *The Hands*: how you act, create momentum, and move through ambiguity without waiting for conditions that may never arrive. And *The Soul*: the purpose, values, courage, and resilience that anchor you when everything around you is in motion.

Navigate is the outer work. The Head, Heart, Hands, and Soul are the foundation you carry into it. What changes is the terrain. You are no longer working on yourself in isolation. You are standing in the room with other people who are navigating change. Part II moves from who you are to how you lead others through the most complex and human dimensions of change. It does not offer a methodology or a step-by-step process, because change does not happen that way. It offers something more useful: an honest examination of what happens when change meets people, and what the most effective change leaders do in those moments.

Apply is where everything comes together in the context of the world we are now leading in. Part III addresses the realities of a disruptive, technology-driven, and rapidly shifting landscape, and what it demands of change leaders who intend to remain relevant, effective, and deeply human in the decades ahead.

This book is for anyone who leads change. Not only those with change management in their title. If you lead a team, a project, an organization, or a community through any kind of shift, this book is for you. If you sit between strategy and delivery, carrying the emotional weight of both, this book is for you. If you have ever stood in a room full of resistant, exhausted, or anxious people and known that the technical answer is not the only answer needed, this book is for you.

Each chapter ends with a journal section. These prompts are not exercises to be completed and forgotten. They are invitations to reflect on what the chapter stirred in you, what it confirmed, what it challenged, and what you will carry into the next room you lead in.

You will encounter stories in these pages that you may have heard before. Shackleton on the ice. Mulally at Ford. The fall of Blockbuster and the reinvention of IBM. I have chosen them deliberately. Change leadership is not a discipline that rewards novelty for its own sake. It rewards pattern recognition. The stories that endure in this field endure because they contain truths that have not yet been fully extracted. I return to them not to retell them, but to read them differently, through the specific lens of the anatomy this book proposes, and to surface what I believe has been consistently overlooked in their conventional teaching. The most familiar story, examined through a new question, often yields the most unexpected insight.

The world needs change leaders who see human beings beyond organizational charts. Who understand that every project plan contains people, and that those people are carrying more than anyone sees. Who know when to slow down and when to move fast, and have the wisdom to tell the difference.

That is the change leader this book is for.

PART I
DISCOVER

01

The Head

> *"The very essence of leadership is that you have to have vision. You can't blow an uncertain trumpet."*
> **Theodore Hesburgh**

In the anatomy of a successful change leader, the Head represents clarity, vision, and strategic thinking. It guides how leaders interpret complexity, make decisions, and articulate direction. The Head is not simply intellectual power. It is the disciplined thinking required to shape meaning in times of uncertainty. It is where confusion is transformed into coherence, and where intention becomes direction.

Every change begins first in the mind. Before the plans, the meetings, or the project outlines, a change leader must pause long enough to understand *what is shifting, what is possible, and what matters most.* We often imagine vision in leadership as something dramatic or inspirational, yet it begins quietly, in moments of reflection, curiosity, and deliberate thought. In times of disruption, the ability to think clearly is not a luxury. It is a strategic advantage.

The Head functions much like a GPS. Even the most well-built vehicle cannot move without a clear destination. A GPS does not remove obstacles, but it provides orientation: *where you are, where you are going, and what direction to take next.* When people do not know the destination, resistance grows.

Research suggests that under conditions of uncertainty, brain regions associated with threat detection become more active. When clarity is present, the regions associated with focused attention and decision-making tend to re-engage. For the change leader, this means clarity is not a message to craft. It is a discipline to develop. One that, when carried into a room, changes the conditions for everyone in it. People begin to calm, focus, and engage.

When the environment is uncertain, the Head becomes more essential than ever. With continuous technological advancements, an ever-changing workplace, economic unpredictability, constant organizational restructuring, and geopolitical upheaval, people look to leaders to help them make sense of change. Vision is not ornamental. It is not something added to the beginning of a presentation for inspiration. It is the anchor people hold onto when everything around them feels in motion. A powerful vision answers three questions:

Where are we going?
Why are we going there?
What will be better when we arrive?

Without these answers, change becomes mechanical rather than meaningful. When a person understands the why, there is a shift from compliance to commitment. Compliance sounds like, "I'll do it because I'm told to." Commitment sounds like, "I'll do it because I believe in it." And commitment that leads to collaboration drives ownership.

I remember facilitating a critical kickoff meeting during a large-scale change where every conversation was tactical. Each leader debated challenges, the impact to their business, the pros and cons of the change, cost, timelines, and milestones. The room was filled with activity but no alignment. At one point, I asked, "Does this change align with the organization's goals for where we want to be in the next five years?" The room went silent. In that silence, it became clear that there was no shared definition of success.

I am reminded of the parable of the Blind Men and the Elephant, an ancient parable and one of the most accurate pictures of what happens inside almost every change initiative I have ever seen

The person holding the tail is certain it is a rope. The person at the leg is equally certain it is a tree. The person holding the trunk is convinced it is a snake. The person touching the ear believes it is a fan. The person holding the tusk insists it is a spear. The person touching the body is sure it is a wall.

None of them are wrong. They each had an incomplete view. Now replace the elephant with your change.

The IT leader sees a systems problem. The HR director sees a people problem. The finance lead sees a cost problem. The frontline manager sees a workload problem. The executive sponsor sees an execution problem. Everyone is touching the same change. Everyone is experiencing a different animal.

This is one of the most common reasons change stalls. People are working hard, but not together. When the leaders in the kickoff meeting re-centred around the shared purpose, everything began to shift, not because the issues changed, but because the thinking did.

When Satya Nadella stepped in as CEO of Microsoft, the organization was struggling with identity and internal fractures. Nadella did not begin with restructuring. He began with reframing. His vision, "To empower every person and every organization on the planet to achieve more" was simple, memorable, and transformative. It unified a fragmented company and restored long-term strategic clarity. The thinking changed first. Everything else followed.

The Head is also critical in the work of sensemaking, the change leader's responsibility in helping others interpret complex situations. People often assume resistance comes from ignorance or stubbornness, but more often it comes from cognitive overload. When people cannot make sense of what is happening, they freeze, disengage, or revert to old habits. Sensemaking helps people reclaim their footing. It provides a coherent narrative that answers: *What does this mean? What should I pay attention to? How should I interpret what is happening?*

A change leader's mind works something like an air traffic controller. They are not flying every plane, but they must keep the entire landscape in view, know which movements require immediate attention, and communicate with sufficient precision for others to act with confidence. Sensemaking is that kind of clarity in motion. It does not simplify what is complex. It helps people find their bearings within it.

Change leaders also understand systems rather than symptoms. Many organizations make the mistake of solving surface-level issues without addressing deeper causes. The result is a cycle of fixes that never quite fix anything.

Consider this scenario. A large financial services firm implements a new technology system intended to improve operational efficiency across its customer-facing teams. Adoption is persistently low. Leadership cycles through explanations: inadequate training, poor communication, gaps in process design. Each explanation leads to a new intervention. None of them works. The real issue is something none of those interventions has touched. The system has been designed for efficiency. The frontline teams it is handed to need tools for relationship-building. Those two things are not the same, and no amount of training or communication will close that gap.

The system addresses a process problem, not a human one. It is the organizational equivalent of rearranging the furniture in a burning building. Once leadership can reframe the vision to focus on improving the client experience, adoption can grow. The lesson is simple: you cannot solve a problem you have not understood, and you cannot understand a problem if you only look at the surface.

Systems thinking helps change leaders understand organizational interdependence. When one part of the system shifts, others are affected. Leaders who think in systems anticipate unintended consequences, connect decisions to their ripple effects, and resist the temptation to treat complex problems with simple fixes.

Clarity also requires the discipline of simplification. The world we operate in has never been more VUCA - Volatile, Uncertain, Complex, and Ambiguous, a framework first developed by the U.S. Army War College to describe the post-Cold War world, and one that has found its way into every corner of leadership thinking since. In this environment, complexity can masquerade as sophistication. But in my experience, complexity more often signals confusion. What I have learned over time is that the goal is not to overwhelm people with information. It is to help them make sense of it, the right amount, at the right time. I adopted a simple rule: if I cannot articulate the vision in a few clear sentences, I am not yet ready to lead it.

But even the clearest vision is meaningless if it does not influence how people act. Direction must cascade through the organization. I often use what I call the **Clarity Cascade**: anchor the vision, translate the why, prioritize the what, guide the how, and reinforce consistently.

It is not enough to communicate the vision once. People do not remember what leaders say. They remember what leaders repeat. People need to encounter a message multiple times across multiple channels before it genuinely registers. Aim to say it more than once, across more than one channel. Not because people are not listening, but because people are busy, distracted, and processing change at different speeds. **Repetition is not redundancy. It is how meaning takes root.**

Communication is the engine of clarity. Effective communication is consistent, concise, honest, forward-looking, and two-way. *Consistency* reduces anxiety. *Conciseness* keeps people focused. *Honesty* builds trust. *Forward-looking* communication prepares people for what lies ahead. And *two-way* communication, listening with emotional intelligence, helps leaders uncover misunderstandings before they become roadblocks.

Decision-making is also central to the Head dimension. Change leadership requires making decisions under pressure, with incomplete information, competing priorities, and high expectations. It requires critical thinking and the flexibility to adapt as circumstances evolve. Leaders will never have perfect information. What matters is the ability to make thoughtful decisions aligned with purpose and principles. Two common traps undermine decision-making in change: the perfection trap, waiting too long to act, and the reaction trap, acting too quickly to relieve discomfort. The balance is thoughtful action.

I learned this lesson repeatedly throughout my own journey of leading change, facilitating change leadership programmes, and building the Change Leadership Conference. It is easy to believe expertise means having answers. Over time, I discovered it meant having confidence in my thinking. It meant trusting my internal compass, pausing to interpret rather than rushing to react, and recognizing that the strongest decisions are rarely made alone. The Head is not fixed. It deepens as a leader grows.

When the Head is clear, the Heart can connect, the Hands can take action, and the Soul can anchor the change leader in purpose. Clarity creates alignment. Alignment creates confidence. Confidence creates momentum. The most successful change leaders do not begin with action or emotion. They begin with a thought, with observing patterns, diagnosing meaning, and defining direction. The Head transforms the messy middle of change into coherence, and change leaders into the kind of visionaries that people choose to follow.

YOUR CHANGE LEADER JOURNAL

One Key Takeaway What resonated most with me about clarity, vision, or strategic thinking?

What Might Hold Me Back What beliefs or habits might limit my ability to lead with clarity?

The Action I Am Committed to Taking What is one step I can take to sharpen my clarity or refine my vision?

One Simple Step I Can Take Today Write my one-sentence WHY for the change I am leading, and refine it until it becomes focused and simple.

02

The Heart

"I've learned that people will forget what you said, people will forget what you did, but people will never forget how you made them feel."
Maya Angelou

If the Head provides clarity and direction, the Heart creates connection, belonging, and trust. It is the part of leadership that speaks to humanity and the lived experience of change. Where the Head interprets complexity, the Heart interprets people, their motivations, fears, hopes, and reactions. In every change, people follow leaders not only because they understand the vision, but because they feel understood by the person casting it. Without the Heart, even the most compelling strategy struggles to gain traction.

Empathy, emotional intelligence, and connection are often mislabelled as soft skills, yet they are among the most powerful predictors of effective change leadership.

Leaders who demonstrate empathy consistently build higher-performing teams, foster greater engagement, reduce resistance, and create cultures capable of navigating uncertainty.

Emotional intelligence enables leaders to read the room, understand reactions, regulate their responses, and build relationships that withstand pressure. These capabilities do not eliminate the challenges of change, but they significantly influence how people move through them.

The Heart functions much like a bridge between strategy and execution. It turns plans into partnerships. It transforms directives into dialogue. Without this bridge, people may understand what is being asked of them but feel no desire to participate. There is a saying that has circulated through leadership for generations: "People don't care how much you know until they know how much you care." Leaders may have expertise or authority, but their influence begins with connection.

The science behind connection helps explain why the Heart matters so deeply. Some researchers propose that the brain contains cells that respond when we observe others, helping us interpret the emotions and intentions of those around us.

A leader's anxiety becomes the team's anxiety.
A leader's calm becomes the team's calm.
A leader's empathy signals psychological safety.

Harvard researcher Amy Edmondson identifies psychological safety as the cornerstone of high-performing, adaptive teams. In the context of change, that insight becomes especially important. The Heart is not sentimental. It is fundamentally strategic.

Think of it this way. A change leader's emotional state becomes the weather of the team. People do not debate the weather. They dress for it. They plan around it. They feel it before they name it. When the leader brings calm, the team finds its footing. When the leader brings a storm, the team braces. This is not a metaphor alone. It is the lived reality of every team navigating change under pressure.

I have witnessed the value of having emotional intelligence many times in my career, but one moment remains especially vivid. During a large transformation project, a well-respected but notoriously challenging stakeholder erupted in frustration during a meeting. Their words were sharp. Their tone was heated. The room tensed. In that moment, I had a choice: respond defensively or respond empathetically. I paused, paced myself, and asked quietly, *"What can I do to help right now?"* Their anger dissolved.

What surfaced instead was the fear of losing control, of being excluded, of not being able to effectively support their team through the change. That moment of acknowledgment changed our relationship entirely. They became one of the strongest champions of the change, not because I convinced them with facts, but because I connected with their humanity.

Practicing emotional intelligence requires discipline and self-leadership. *Self-awareness* that helps change leaders recognize their emotional triggers. *Self-management* that enables them to regulate their responses rather than react to them. *Social awareness* that equips them to read the emotional climate of a room and respond with intention rather than instinct. These are not innate traits. They are learnable skills that grow with deliberate and consistent practice.

In a world of constant change, filled with ambiguity, complexity and uncertainty, emotional intelligence can become a change leader's greatest advantage. It is the ability to be aware of and manage your own emotions, while understanding and navigating the emotions of others, and in service of the best possible outcome for everyone involved.

One of the most frequently named challenges for change leaders is resistance, and this is where the Heart becomes particularly important. Resistance is often framed as opposition, but it is better understood as information. It signals fear, uncertainty, or unaddressed needs. Leaders who rely only on the Head may see resistance as a barrier to overcome. Leaders who lead with the Heart interpret resistance as an opportunity to understand. In one digital transformation I supported, a group of long-tenured employees were labelled as "negative" and "difficult." But when I invited them into a conversation, their resistance came from deep loyalty to the organization and genuine concern about losing the human-centred practices that had defined their work. Once the leaders acknowledged those fears, resistance started to shift into advocacy.

Conflict is also inevitable in change. Change leaders who avoid conflict create environments where issues remain unresolved and voices go unheard. Leaders who rush into resolving conflict without empathy risk escalating tension. The Heart enables change leaders to approach conflict with curiosity rather than judgment. A simple shift from "What's the issue?" to "What's important to you about this?" transforms conversations by uncovering values rather than debating positions.

Genuine understanding lowers defensiveness and clears the path toward collaboration.

The Heart plays a critical role in how change leaders guide people through the emotional terrain of change. People do not move through change in a straight line. They experience it as a journey of emotions, often cycling through excitement, resistance, grief, confusion, fatigue, and hope, often in ways that defy any predictable sequence. This emotional journey is what practitioners refer to as the *change curve*, a framework drawn from two distinct bodies of work: Elisabeth Kübler-Ross's foundational research on grief and loss, which was later adapted by change practitioners for organizational contexts, and William Bridges's work on transition, which specifically addressed how people navigate the psychological journey through change. Together, they have shaped one of the most widely used frameworks for understanding the human emotional experience of change.

Logic alone cannot move people through that emotional terrain. Change leaders must acknowledge discomfort, validate experience, and offer steadiness. During a culture change initiative I was leading, an executive I coached learned this firsthand during a town hall. Their initial message emphasized efficiency and innovation, but employees were quietly terrified about job security. The second town hall began differently: "I know this is unsettling, and I have had my own moments of uncertainty." That honesty shifted the emotional tone entirely. People listened differently because they felt seen.

Trust, too, is central to the Heart. Change tests trust, sometimes straining it considerably. Trust fractures occur when communication is unclear, when decisions feel unfair, or when people feel excluded. Repairing trust requires focusing on impact, not intention. Leaders often respond to tension by explaining what they meant or defending their choices. But trust is rebuilt when change leaders acknowledge how people feel: "I see how that landed, and I'm sorry for the impact it had." One leader I worked with during restructuring learned this the hard way. Their team interpreted the silence as bad news. In the absence of communication, people will always write their own ending, and it is rarely an optimistic one. When the leader finally addressed the team, their first instinct was to explain and defend rather than acknowledge. That defensiveness deepened the anxiety in the room. When they shifted to acknowledgment, the air cleared almost immediately.

In diverse and hybrid workplaces, empathy and emotional intelligence require intentionality. Change leaders must also understand how cultural backgrounds shape emotional expression, how introverts and extroverts experience change differently, and how remote employees may feel disconnected during transitions. Empathy becomes a cross-cultural leadership skill. It helps leaders suspend assumptions, learn from differences, and create inclusive change experiences where every person feels seen.

A change leader's willingness to have difficult conversations, sit with discomfort, acknowledge not knowing, and show vulnerability without losing authority makes all the difference. Brené Brown's research reminds us that vulnerability is not weakness. It is the foundation of courageous leadership. Change leaders who show up authentically create environments where others feel permission to be authentic too.

Self-compassion is equally essential. This is where an important distinction is worth naming. The emotional labour of leading change is heavy, and it is easy to absorb the weight of those around you. The most sustainable form of empathy for a change leader is cognitive empathy, understanding what others are feeling and why, rather than compassionate empathy, which involves taking those feelings on as your own. One equips you to lead. The other risks depleting you. This distinction is one of the most practically important insights a change leader can have. Leading with the Heart begins with recognizing your own humanity, your triggers, your fatigue, your boundaries, and your needs. When change leaders understand their own internal landscape, they regulate more effectively and support others more sustainably.

> Change leaders with a strong emotional presence create calm amid chaos, safety amid ambiguity, and confidence amid uncertainty.

The Heart is what enables leaders to bring people along the journey, not through pressure, but through connection. When the Heart is present, people feel respected, valued, and understood. They are more willing to take risks, engage honestly, and participate in change. The Heart is not separate from the Head. It amplifies it. Together, they create the foundation for change that is not only strategic, but human.

YOUR CHANGE LEADER JOURNAL

One Key Takeaway What insight about empathy, emotional intelligence, or connection resonated most with me?

What Might Hold Me Back What emotional habits, assumptions, or triggers might limit my ability to lead with empathy?

The Action I Am Committed to Taking What specific steps will I take to strengthen emotional connection with my team, peers, or stakeholders?

One Simple Step I Can Take Today I will choose one person affected by a change and ask: 'How is this impacting you?' I will listen without interrupting.

03

The Hands

"You don't have to see the whole staircase, just take the first step."

Martin Luther King Jr.

If the Head offers clarity and the Heart builds connection, the Hands turn possibility into progress. The Hands represent action, execution, influence, experimentation, and agility. They are the part of leadership responsible for moving ideas out of strategy decks and into the real world. Leadership without action is philosophy. Action without leadership is chaos. The Hands bring intention to life.

Only action creates movement. *"Vision without execution is hallucination."* A line widely attributed to Thomas Edison. Leaders often underestimate how critical it is to show progress early, consistently, and visibly. People do not commit to change because the plan is impressive. They commit because they can see it taking shape.

The Hands function like the engine of a change. A beautifully designed car will not move without its engine. A strategic change plan, no matter how compelling, remains motionless without the power of action behind it. Engines do not operate on inspiration. They operate on pressure, ignition, and movement. In the same way, the Hands drive change by converting thought and intention into tangible steps that people can see and experience.

Action in change leadership should inspire confidence and build credibility. It is purposeful, intentional, and aligned with the Head's vision and the Heart's connection. Effective action is less about volume and more about direction. It is easy to mistake a completed list of tasks for meaningful progress, when in reality, busyness can quietly conceal the absence of real movement. The Hands demand discernment, deciding not only what to do, but what not to do, and when to do it.

In change leadership, action must be both strategic and agile. Change leaders need to move quickly enough to maintain momentum, but not so quickly that they leave people behind or create unnecessary chaos. Speed without direction is not progress. It is risk. Change leaders must make decisions with incomplete information, knowing that genuine progress often requires learning through doing rather than waiting until every variable is known. The Hands embody this balance.

Neuroscience underscores the importance of early action. Research by Harvard professors Teresa Amabile and Steven Kramer, captured in their book The Progress Principle, shows that individuals and teams experience their highest levels of motivation when they see visible progress toward meaningful goals. Not massive progress. Small, consistent steps. This behavioural finding is reinforced by neuroscience research showing that progress activates the brain's reward pathways, sustaining motivation and building momentum over time. It moves them from skepticism to belief, from fear to curiosity, from hesitation to commitment.

This principle plays out in every change initiative. When people see early wins, even small ones, confidence grows. When they see nothing but meetings, plans, and discussions, or there is a lack of engagement, doubt spreads. One visible action can shift the emotional climate more powerfully than a dozen presentations.

A vivid example of this principle comes from Franklin D. Roosevelt's leadership during the Great Depression. When he took office, fear and uncertainty were pervasive. Rather than waiting for perfect solutions, Roosevelt focused on immediate action, stabilizing the banking system, rolling out small but visible relief programs, and communicating through his fireside chats. These actions did not instantly resolve the crisis, but they changed the national mood. They signaled leadership. They demonstrated that progress was possible. The country began to believe again because it could see movement.

This pattern repeats across industries and across generations. When change leaders take early action, they build credibility. When they wait too long for perfect conditions, they lose momentum. The Hands remind us that leaders are judged not by what they know, but by what they do.

In organizations, action is not just the leader's responsibility. It is the leader's influence. People look to leaders not for tasks but for signals. When change leaders model action, others follow. When change leaders stall, others wait. Influence is amplified by behaviour far more than by instruction. Change momentum works like a row of dominoes. The first one does not need to be the largest or the most perfectly placed. It simply needs to fall. Once it does, the energy released is greater than the energy required to start it. Leaders who wait for the perfect first move often find that the row has already begun to topple around them, without their hand on it.

Influence in change leadership is built on three qualities working together: *visible action, consistent action, and aligned action.* Visible action helps people see movement. Consistent action reassures people that progress will not fade after the first announcement. Aligned action shows that decisions reflect the vision and values that leaders speak about. When these three qualities converge, influence becomes natural rather than forced.

Influence is also shaped by how leaders make decisions. In environments dominated by change, leaders often face incomplete information. Waiting for certainty can stall momentum, but acting prematurely can create chaos. The Hands require leaders to navigate that tension with flexibility and adaptability. Change is not static. Today's challenges are complex and often require multidimensional responses rather than linear solutions. Change leaders must create space for testing assumptions, gathering feedback, and adjusting strategies as understanding deepens. This is not indecision. It is intelligent iteration.

Leading change today requires agility, and agility requires both courage and humility. Courage to move forward without perfect information. Humility to correct course without shame or defensiveness. Leaders who embody the Hands know that change is iterative, not linear. They trust the process of learning through doing. Agility also means learning from setbacks. No change initiative unfolds exactly as planned. Leaders who respond to setbacks with transparency and adaptability strengthen trust. Leaders who react with defensiveness or blame undermine it. The Hands require leaders to treat setbacks as data, and every course correction as evidence that they are paying attention.

Action also reveals misalignment. A plan may look flawless on paper, but it may encounter unexpected resistance when it meets reality. Taking action exposes gaps early and provides the insight needed to adjust before those gaps become crises. Leaders who avoid action avoid reality.

> Change leaders who embrace action learn faster, adapt faster, and build the kind of credibility that no presentation can manufacture.

Action also plays a central role in clearing obstacles. Change leaders who remove barriers, whether procedural, cultural, or structural, demonstrate commitment in tangible ways. Teams or stakeholders feel supported. Work accelerates. One of the fastest ways a change leader builds credibility is to eliminate a bottleneck that has been quietly draining momentum.

But action alone is not enough. Sustaining execution over time requires focus. Change efforts often lose momentum not because leaders lack vision or empathy, but because they fail to manage competing priorities, capacity constraints, and fatigue. Layer on the constant external forces driving disruption, from technology to socioeconomic and geopolitical pressures, and the weight compounds. Change fatigue emerges when the emotional and cognitive load of sustained change becomes heavier than people can carry without support. It is not resistance. It is exhaustion.

Change leaders can address fatigue by communicating consistently, clarifying priorities, managing capacity realistically, and spotlighting small wins. Clear priorities help teams make decisions without confusion. Realistic capacity management prevents burnout. Celebrating small wins reinforces positive momentum and reminds people that their efforts are producing real results. These practices keep teams engaged and empowered throughout the full arc of the change journey, not just at the beginning when energy is highest.

In an organization I supported during a major change, the team began to feel overwhelmed by the volume and duration of the work. In response, we introduced a monthly project bulletin where teams regularly shared one small accomplishment related to the change. Each edition included a message from a different leader and recognized the contributions of specific teams. The atmosphere shifted noticeably. People began to see movement instead of obstacles. They recognized their own capability rather than their limitations. Small wins became psychological fuel that kept the larger journey moving.

Momentum depends not only on movement but on belief. People follow leaders who help them see that their efforts matter and that progress is being made. Change leaders who narrate progress, highlighting improvements, sharing updates, and reinforcing direction, strengthen collective confidence in ways that strategy documents never can.

Ultimately, the Hands represent change leadership in motion, leadership experienced, not proclaimed. Your actions reveal your values. They communicate your courage. They define your influence. A change leader who consistently takes aligned, visible, and thoughtful action becomes credible, trusted, and genuinely influential.

Change leadership is ultimately expressed through what you do. The Hands ensure that what you do builds a future worth following.

YOUR CHANGE LEADER JOURNAL

One Key Takeaway What insight about action, influence, or agility stood out to me most?

What Might Hold Me Back What habits, fears, or perfectionist tendencies could limit my ability to take bold action?

The Action I Am Committed to Taking What one meaningful step can I take to move the change I'm leading forward?

One Simple Step I Can Take Today I will identify one block slowing my team down and remove it.

04

The Soul

"He who has a why to live can bear almost any how."

Friedrich Nietzsche

Every change leader carries something within them that cannot be taught in a classroom or captured in a methodology. It is deeper than skill, broader than knowledge, and more enduring than experience. It is the Soul.

It is the place where purpose lives, where courage is formed, where values take shape, and where resilience is strengthened. **Purpose, courage, values, and resilience are not separate qualities.** They are the four expressions of a single inner foundation, and together they define who a change leader is at their core.

If the Head provides clarity, the Heart creates connection, and the Hands drive action, the Soul is what sustains leaders when clarity fades, when connection feels strained, and when action becomes difficult. It is the centre that holds everything together.

The Soul functions like an anchor. It does not calm the storm around a change leader, and it does not remove the difficulty of the journey. But it holds the leader in place when everything around them is in motion. Without it, leaders do not collapse suddenly. They drift. Slowly, almost imperceptibly, until one day they look up and realize they are somewhere they never intended to be.

The Soul is the dimension of leadership that asks not "What are we doing?" or "How will we do it?" but "Why does this matter?" and "Who do I choose to be in this moment?" These questions require introspection, honesty, and humility. They require a change leader to anchor themselves in something deeper than outcomes, something that does not collapse when circumstances shift.

I have led change initiatives that tested me in ways I did not anticipate. Highly charged stakeholders, tense moments, political dynamics, and situations that pushed me to question whether I could continue in good conscience. There were times I was prepared to walk away from a project entirely because of integrity issues. What kept me centred through all of it was a clear and unwavering sense of why. Purpose is not something I talk about in theory. It is the thing that has held me steady when everything else felt uncertain.

Purpose is often misunderstood in leadership. It is not merely a grand statement about changing the world or an aspirational slogan crafted during a planning session. Purpose is personal. It is the internal compass that guides a leader's decisions, shapes their behaviours, and grounds them during uncertainty. Purpose gives direction when external markers disappear. It is what keeps leaders standing when challenges mount and when outcomes are not immediate.

Change leadership tests purpose relentlessly. There will be days when progress feels slow, when resistance is strong, when stakeholders doubt your message, or when your own confidence trembles. Without a clear sense of purpose, leaders can become reactive, discouraged, or disconnected. But when purpose is strong, leaders remain centred. They make decisions anchored in meaning rather than fear. They hold to the path even when it becomes steep.

Courage in leadership is rooted in the Soul. Courage is often romanticized, but in practice it is rarely glamorous.

It is quiet, internal, and deeply personal. Courage shows up not in dramatic gestures, but in steady, consistent choices. The choice to speak truthfully when silence would be easier. To make a difficult decision when popularity is at stake. To take the next step when the outcome is uncertain. Courage is not the absence of fear but the willingness to act despite it.

History is full of change leaders who embodied this type of courage. Nelson Mandela demonstrated extraordinary courage by choosing to fight for freedom, and after his release from prison, to pursue reconciliation over revenge, a decision that reshaped a nation. Malala Yousafzai showed courage by speaking for girls' education despite her life being repeatedly at stake. But courage also exists in everyday leadership: the manager who stands up for their team, the senior leader who admits they do not have all the answers, the project lead who challenges assumptions to protect people's well-being. Courage does not require a global stage. It requires only the willingness to choose integrity over comfort.

Values form the third dimension of the Soul. Values are not abstract ideals. They are behavioural commitments. They determine how change leaders make choices when no one is watching and how they respond when the pressure mounts. Values shape the quality of leadership because they influence whether leaders stay aligned with integrity or drift into convenience. During times of change, values are tested more intensely than at any other time. It becomes tempting to compromise, justify, or take shortcuts. Values anchor change leaders against wavering, even when the pressure to compromise feels strong. This is the consistency that builds trust and stability, something teams and stakeholders can depend on when everything else feels uncertain.

Resilience lives in the Soul. It is not toughness or endurance alone. It is the ability to recover, refocus, and re-engage, and it is built quietly over time in the moments most leaders would rather forget. Think of a tree in a storm. The branches bend dramatically, sometimes to the point where you are certain something will break. But the root system, invisible and underground, holds. Resilience is that root system. It is built long before the storm arrives, in the quiet ordinary moments of leading with integrity and intention. Change leadership demands it because change is unpredictable, emotionally taxing, and rarely linear. Setbacks, resistance, fatigue, and moments of genuine self-doubt are not exceptions to the journey. They are part of it.

Resilience is what allows change leaders to encounter all of this without losing perspective, without crumbling under pressure, and without losing sight of why they started.

That capacity begins from within. The Soul is where personal identity intersects with professional responsibility. Every change leader brings their story, background, beliefs, and experiences into their leadership. These elements influence how they interpret challenges, respond to pressure, and engage with others. The Soul requires leaders to explore this inner landscape honestly. It invites them to reflect on questions such as:

What shaped me?
What strengths have carried me this far?
What fears limit my decisions?
Where do I derive my confidence?

The Soul is not about perfection. It is about awareness. It is about understanding what fuels you and what derails you. It is about identifying the values you want to embody and the type of change leader you aspire to be. When change leaders develop this awareness, they stand more firmly, move more confidently, and lead more authentically.

What I have noticed most consistently throughout my change leadership journey is this: the change leaders who thrive know themselves well. They have done the inner work, and it shows. They know who they are, what matters to them, and how they want to lead. This self-knowledge does not make them rigid. It makes them grounded. They are open to learning but are not easily swayed by pressure. They adapt without losing themselves. They act with conviction because their decisions are anchored in something stable.

I recall coaching a senior leader who was navigating a complex organizational restructuring. They were competent, respected, and strategic. But beneath the surface, they struggled with the fear of disappointing people. This fear led to hesitation, delayed decisions, and emotional exhaustion. Through coaching, they reconnected with their why: their purpose as a leader, their values around fairness and transparency, and their belief in empowering others. Once they aligned their decisions with these deeper anchors, their leadership shifted. They communicated with more clarity, made decisions with confidence, and gained credibility because they were leading from an authentic centre rather than from fear.

Purpose becomes real only when it is lived. Leaders often speak passionately about their purpose in moments of calm, but it is in moments of pressure that purpose reveals its true strength. When decisions become difficult, when resistance intensifies, or when outcomes are uncertain, purpose acts as a stabilizer. It helps leaders stay anchored in what matters rather than getting swept into reactivity or confusion. Purpose helps leaders make choices that align with who they want to be, not just what circumstances demand.

Ursula Burns, former CEO of Xerox and the first Black woman to lead a Fortune 500 company, offers a powerful example. Burns grew up in public housing, and her purpose was anchored in expanding opportunity. Her decisions reflected this purpose: investing in people, challenging limiting beliefs, and creating pathways for underrepresented talent. Her leadership was not driven by optics. It was guided by conviction.

Courage is closely tied to purpose because courage is the willingness to act in alignment with purpose despite fear. Leaders who act courageously often experience internal tension before they experience clarity. They feel the discomfort of risking approval or reputation. They feel the weight of others' expectations. Yet they act based on values, not fear.

Paul Polman's leadership at Unilever illustrates this precisely. When he shifted the company away from short-term shareholder priorities toward long-term sustainability, investors resisted, and critics questioned his direction. But Polman remained steadfast because his purpose was stronger than the pressure. Over time, Unilever thrived, not just economically but reputationally, becoming one of the most cited examples of purpose-driven leadership in the world.

Values sit at the foundation of these decisions. They guide leaders through complexity by serving as a reliable compass. Change leaders grounded in values create psychological safety. They communicate with consistency. They treat people with dignity. They build organizations that reflect integrity.

The Soul evolves through reflection and practice. It becomes stronger each time change leaders choose integrity over convenience, accountability over avoidance, and courage over fear. It grows when change leaders face uncertainty without losing themselves. It deepens when change leaders respond with intention rather than reaction. The Soul matures when adversity is viewed not as a barrier but as an invitation to rise.

The Soul shapes legacy. People remember leaders for their decisions, but they remember them more for their character, how they treated others, how they handled pressure, and how they showed up during difficult moments. Action may produce immediate results, but leadership rooted in the Soul produces lasting impact.

Change leadership anchored in the Soul is unwavering and sustaining. It provides direction when the path is unclear, strength when circumstances are heavy, and consistency when the environment is changing. When the Head offers clarity, the Heart builds connection, and the Hands create action, it is the Soul that ensures the leader remains whole. The Soul is where identity becomes leadership, and where leadership becomes legacy.

You have now explored the four dimensions of the anatomy of a successful change leader. *The Head, the Heart, the Hands, and the Soul* are not separate concepts. They are interconnected forces that shape how you think, act, lead, and who you choose to be. Together, they form the inner foundation of you as a change leader.

In Part II, we move from Discover to Navigate, from the inner work to the outer work. From who you are as a change leader, to how you lead others through the most complex and human dimensions of change. The playbook begins now.

YOUR CHANGE LEADER JOURNAL

One Key Takeaway Which insight about purpose, courage, values, or resilience resonated most deeply with me?

What Might Hold Me Back Which internal fears, habits, or doubts often pull me away from my Soul?

The Action I Am Committed to Taking What is one intentional step I will commit to taking to lead from my Soul?

One Simple Step I Can Take Today I will identify one value that matters to me and act in alignment with it before the day ends.

PART II
NAVIGATE

05

The Human Side of Change

"People don't resist change. They resist being changed."
Peter Senge

Every change begins with people, yet people are often the part change leaders understand the least. We easily forget that change is for people and led by people. Change leaders can plan for processes, systems, and structures with precision, but the human experience of change resists neat diagrams and predictable timelines. It is nuanced. It is emotional. It is deeply personal. And it is the true ground on which every change succeeds or fails.

You have spent Part I exploring the inner work of being a change leader, the clarity of the Head, the connection of the Heart, the action of the Hands, and the purpose of the Soul. Part II is where that inner foundation meets the outer reality. It is where who you are as a change leader shapes how you lead others through the most complex and human dimensions of change.

Over the years, I have seen leaders, projects, and organizations underestimate this reality. They assemble project plans, build communication strategies, and map out milestones. They believe that if the message is clear enough and the plan is strong enough, people will follow. But change does not happen in presentation decks. It happens within conversations, within feelings, within the subtle shifts of trust and belief. It happens in the space between what people hear and what they internalize. It happens in the gap between what is intended and what people experience.

Leading through the human side of change requires the same awareness a navigator brings to an iceberg. What is visible above the surface, the question, the pushback, the silence, the crossed arms in a meeting, is rarely the whole story. What drives human behaviour during change almost always sits below the waterline. The navigator does not fear the ice they can see. They fear the mass they cannot. Change leaders who learn to look beneath the surface of behaviour find something more human and more workable than what first appeared.

When change leaders fail to account for this human experience, they find themselves frustrated. They think people are "resistant," "difficult," or "slow to adopt." Yet beneath those labels is a simple truth: people are not resisting change. They are responding to uncertainty. They are reacting to what change means for them. And meaning is always emotional before it is logical.

To lead through the human side of change is to commit to seeing what lies beneath the surface. It is to recognize that every behaviour is rooted in a belief, every reaction in a story, and every hesitation in a fear. It is to lead not only with strategy but with empathy, curiosity, and emotional intelligence. This chapter is an invitation to step into that deeper dimension of change leadership.

Human beings are wired for stability. The brain's threat response activates when familiar structures shift, triggering heightened vigilance, anxiety, or avoidance. Change leaders often interpret these responses as resistance, when in reality they are the brain's natural attempts to regain a sense of control. This is why people often process change in emotional waves. At first there may be confusion or disbelief, followed by anxiety, skepticism, exploration, and eventually commitment. These stages do not unfold neatly, nor do they follow a straight line. They loop, overlap, and repeat. Change leaders who understand this pattern approach change not with impatience, but with awareness. They understand that emotions are not obstacles to the work. They are the work.

When people ask, "Why is this happening?" or "How will this affect me?" they are not challenging leadership. They are seeking orientation. When they say, "We tried this before," they are not being negative. They are drawing from memory to make meaning. When they seem disengaged or hesitant, they are often trying to protect themselves from past disappointments or future uncertainty.

Change leadership is not about dismissing these emotions. It is about interpreting them with compassion. A change leader's role is not to push people past their discomfort, but to walk with them through it. It is to create an environment where people feel supported enough to let go of certainty and step into the unknown.

One of the greatest skills of a change leader is the ability to listen beneath what people say. The human side of change rarely reveals itself directly. People often express their fears through questions, frustrations, or silence.

> A change leader's task is to decode the meaning behind the message.

When someone says, "This doesn't make sense," they may be expressing confusion, but more often they are expressing fear: fear of not having a place in the new structure, fear of not being able to keep up, fear of losing influence, identity, or security.

When someone challenges a decision publicly, the issue may not be the decision. It may be a deeper concern about whether change leaders truly understand the impact. And when someone withdraws or avoids engagement, it may not be apathy. It may be self-protection. Change leaders who cultivate emotional intelligence notice the tone beneath the words, the pause before the sentence, the tension in the body, the weariness in the eyes. They pick up the unspoken. They respond not to the symptoms, but to the source.

Over two decades of change work, I have noticed that resistance tends to express itself in a small number of recognizable patterns, each of which signals something different beneath the surface.

Learning to read these patterns is one of the most practical skills a change leader can develop:

When someone asks repeated questions that have already been answered, they are rarely seeking information. They are seeking reassurance. The question beneath the question is almost always: am I going to be okay?

When someone agrees enthusiastically in the meeting and does nothing afterward, they are not being dishonest. They are navigating a gap between what they feel safe to say publicly and what they believe privately. The behaviour signals that psychological safety in the room is lower than it appears.

When someone becomes unusually focused on process, detail, or procedure, they are often trying to regain a sense of control in an environment that feels uncontrollable. The rigidity is not about the process. It is about the uncertainty.

When someone withdraws, becomes quieter than usual, or stops attending optional meetings, they are not disengaged. They are conserving energy. This is often the earliest sign that the emotional weight of the change is becoming heavier than they can carry.

And when someone becomes openly critical or confrontational, particularly someone who was previously collaborative, they are almost always protecting something they have not yet been invited to name. The confrontation is the surface. The vulnerability is underneath.

None of these patterns require a dramatic intervention. They require a change leader who notices them, interprets them with curiosity rather than frustration, and responds to what is underneath rather than what is visible.

This kind of listening communicates something essential:

I see you. I hear you. You matter.

In times of change, this is often the one thing people need most.

I want to tell you about a moment that changed the way I lead. Several years ago, I was brought into a large-scale change initiative as the change lead. The initiative was well funded, strategically sound, and had full executive support. By every measure, it should have moved smoothly. But there was one person standing in the way, or so everyone believed.

It was a senior director. Respected and experienced, and by the time I arrived, thoroughly labelled. Difficult. Obstructive. A blocker. People rolled their eyes when the director's name came up in planning meetings. The director had challenged every timeline, questioned every decision, and pushed back on every proposal the team had brought forward. The project lead suggested that if they can't be brought onside, they may need to be escalated around.

I asked for a one-on-one meeting with the director before I did anything else. They arrived guarded. Arms crossed. The kind of body language that signals not hostility, but protection. There is a difference, and it matters. I did not open with data. I did not bring a slide deck or a process map. I simply asked, "Help me understand what this looks like from where you sit."

They looked at me for a long moment, as if deciding whether the question was genuine or a trap. Then something shifted. Their posture softened slightly. And they began to talk. What came out over the next forty minutes was not resistance. It was a story.

Three years earlier, during a previous change at the same organization, their team had been restructured without warning. People they had hired, developed, and fought for lost their roles in a single afternoon. They found out the same way the team did, in a meeting they were not invited to prepare for. They had walked out of that building feeling blindsided, betrayed, and responsible for people they had not been able to protect.

They had never fully processed it. And now, every time a new initiative arrived with the language of change and efficiency and alignment, their nervous system responded as if it were happening again. Their resistance was not about this change. It was about the last one.

Once I understood that, everything changed. Not the project plan. Not the timeline. Not the strategy. What changed was my approach. I stopped trying to bring them onside and started trying to bring them in. I invited them into shaping aspects of the implementation. I gave them information before meetings rather than during them. I checked in privately before anything significant was announced. I acknowledged, out loud and more than once, what had happened before and why this time would be handled differently.

Within six weeks they had become one of the most influential advocates for the change. Not because I convinced them. Because I understood them.

People are not difficult. Their experiences are. And when change leaders take the time to understand the experience, the wall comes down every time.

That experience reaffirmed something I have come to believe more firmly with each passing year of this work: the single most important skill a change leader can develop is not strategic planning, not stakeholder mapping, not communication frameworks. It is the ability to sit with another person's experience without rushing to fix it.

Among all the roles involved in a change, those who sit between strategy and delivery carry the greatest emotional weight. They are the ones people turn to for answers, reassurance, and clarity. They are also the ones senior change leaders look to for execution and alignment. They sit at the intersection of strategy and impact, carrying the concerns of the people around them while remaining accountable for outcomes. These change leaders often feel unprepared for this emotional load. They fear saying the wrong thing. They struggle with their own uncertainties. They worry about supporting others while navigating their own fears about the future. When this reality is overlooked, it creates a silent strain that quietly undermines morale and momentum.

Change leaders at every level require more than just information. They require three essentials.

Clarity: You need to understand the why, the what, and the how before the people around you can internalize it.

Confidence: You must feel competent and supported enough to answer questions without fear of appearing uninformed.

Connection: You need safe spaces to express your own concerns and support one another through the emotional journey.

When you have these three things, whether you are equipping yourself or supporting other change leaders, you become a stabilizer rather than a stress amplifier. You become the steady presence people lean on rather than the source of the anxiety they are already carrying.

Much of the frustration change leaders experience comes from misunderstanding resistance. Resistance is often interpreted as defiance, negativity, or unwillingness. But resistance is not an attack on the change effort. It is an emotional response to uncertainty. At its core, resistance is information. It tells change leaders where people are struggling. It reveals what needs more clarity. It signals where trust may be fragile. It highlights where support is required.

When change leaders view resistance as a threat, they push harder, and walls rise higher. But when they view resistance as a message, they respond with curiosity, not force. They ask deeper questions. They listen differently. They engage with empathy instead of urgency.

> Resistance becomes a doorway, not a barrier. It becomes the beginning of connection rather than the end of cooperation.

The most powerful condition a change leader can create is psychological safety, the belief that people can express questions, concerns, and ideas without fear of judgment or negative consequences.

When Alan Mulally became CEO of Ford in 2006, he inherited a company losing billions of dollars and a leadership culture where admitting problems had become career suicide. In his weekly Business Plan Review meetings, he asked each leader to color-code their projects: green for on track, yellow for caution, red for problems needing attention. For weeks, every single slide came in green. Mulally knew this was impossible. A company hemorrhaging that much money could not have everything on track.

Then one week, Mark Fields, who led Ford's Americas operations, walked in with a red slide. He had a product-launch problem and was naming it publicly. The room went silent. Senior leaders braced for what would come next. Mulally began to clap. "Mark," he said, "that is great visibility." The following week, the room was full of yellow and red slides. Ford's leaders had finally found it safe to tell the truth. That shift became one of the foundations of Ford's remarkable recovery. While General Motors and Chrysler both required government bailouts in 2009, Ford did not. Mulally later reflected that the most important thing he had done was create an environment where people felt safe enough to say what was happening. Not what they hoped was happening, but what was happening.

Psychological safety is not softness. It is the condition under which honest, accurate, and useful information flows. Without it, change leaders are making decisions based on what people are willing to say rather than on what is true. In a psychologically safe environment, people do not hide their confusion. They do not mask their fear. They do not pretend to understand when they do not.

They speak openly, ask questions, and take risks. And when people feel safe to speak, change leaders receive the honest information they need to make better decisions.

Psychological safety does not eliminate discomfort. It does not guarantee agreement. It does not remove the challenges of change. Instead, it provides a foundation of trust that allows people to walk through discomfort with stability.

> Change leaders build psychological safety by being transparent even when answers are incomplete.
>
> *By acknowledging* emotions rather than dismissing them.
>
> *By welcoming* dissent as data, by admitting when they do not know.
>
> *By following* through on commitments.
>
> And *by treating* every voice with respect.

These behaviours communicate something essential:

You are safe here. Your voice matters here. We will walk this together.

When people feel psychologically safe, change is no longer something happening to them. It becomes something they can participate in. And participation is the beginning of ownership. When people feel part of the process, their mindset shifts. They become collaborators, not opponents. The human side of change becomes a shared journey rather than a directive. They feel empowered.

Change is always, at its heart, a human story. Not a process story. Not a technology story. Not a strategy story. A human story. And the change leaders who understand this, who slow down long enough to hear that story, who resist the pull toward plans and frameworks when what the moment calls for is presence and listening, these are the change leaders people choose to follow. Not because they have all the answers. Because they see the person standing in front of them.

YOUR CHANGE LEADER JOURNAL

One Key Takeaway What insight about the human experience of change resonated most deeply with me?

What Might Hold Me Back Which patterns, assumptions, or fears may make it challenging for me to lead through emotion?

The Action I Am Committed to Taking What intentional conversation or moment of listening can I initiate?

One Simple Step I Can Take Today I will ask one person: 'What part of this change feels most challenging right now?' and listen with presence.

06

Influence, Adaptive Leadership, and Navigating Hidden Dynamics

"You can have brilliant ideas, but if you can't get them across, your ideas won't get you anywhere."
Lee Iacocca

I remember being brought in to support a large-scale change initiative that had been stalling for months. On paper everything looked right. The strategy was sound. The executive sponsor was engaged. The project team was experienced and committed. Yet the change was not moving. Meetings were polite but cold. Decisions were made and then quietly unmade. Communication felt careful in a way that suggested people were choosing their words rather than speaking them.

When I spent time with the different people involved, something began to emerge beneath the professional surface. Two senior leaders, both widely respected and genuinely committed to the organization, were navigating a rivalry neither had fully acknowledged. Their departments had historically competed for resources, visibility, and strategic influence. Over the years, a quiet tension had developed, not dramatic enough to name, not minor enough to ignore. And now this change, which required both to collaborate in ways they had never done before, was landing directly on that unresolved history.

Neither of them was obstructing the change deliberately. They were protecting their teams from what they feared the change might cost them. One feared losing the influence their department had spent years building. The other feared being held accountable for outcomes they did not feel they had shaped. Their behaviour in meetings, the delayed responses, the carefully worded concerns, and the reluctance to commit were not resistance to the change itself. It was protection of something they were not yet ready to name out loud.

I had individual conversations with each of them before doing anything else. Not to negotiate. Not to present data or make a case. Simply to understand what each of them was carrying.

What those conversations revealed changed my entire approach. Each leader, when given space to speak without the pressure of the room, named a version of the same fear. They were not sure their concerns had been genuinely heard. They were not sure the change had been designed with their people's reality in mind. And beneath all of it, neither of them was confident the other would act in good faith when it mattered most.

I did not bring them together for a dramatic resolution. That is not how organizational dynamics work. What I did instead was change how I worked with each of them individually. I shared information with each of them earlier and before meetings, rather than during. I created opportunities for each of them to shape aspects of the implementation that mattered most to their teams. I acknowledged, privately and more than once, the history between the two departments and why the trust gap was understandable rather than a personal failure. I stopped trying to manage the dynamic from the outside and started working within it, meeting each person where they were rather than where I needed them to be.

The shift did not happen in a single conversation. It happened gradually, almost imperceptibly, over several weeks. Decisions started moving. Information started flowing more freely. The careful, guarded atmosphere in the meetings began to change. Neither leader ever fully named what had changed. But they both began to act differently, and that was what mattered.

I tell this story because it illustrates something I have come to believe more firmly with each year leading change and working with organizations. The most common reason change stalls is not the strategy. It is not the plan. It is not even the resistance. It is the unspoken dynamics operating beneath the surface of every meeting, every email, and every politely worded concern. And the change leaders who learn to read and navigate those dynamics are the ones who move things forward when everyone else has run out of explanations for why nothing is happening. This is the heart of influence and adaptive leadership.

Influence remains one of the most misunderstood words in organizations. People associate it with charisma, with seniority, with political savvy, with position, or with the ability to convince people of things they would not otherwise believe. But real influence, the kind that moves change forward in sustainable and meaningful ways, is none of those things. Real influence is trust made visible. It is the accumulated credibility of every commitment kept, every difficult conversation handled with integrity, every moment where one small shift is made.

In many organizations where I have worked, there is a quiet truth that rarely appears in job descriptions or competency frameworks. Change does not happen because someone has a title or because a mandate has been issued. Change happens because someone has influence. And some of the most powerful influencers in any organization are people whose titles do not begin to reflect the magnitude of their impact. I have met coordinators who could mobilize an entire department with a single conversation. I have seen mid-level change leaders unlock alignment that senior executives had been unable to achieve for months. These individuals were not successful because of where they sat in the hierarchy. They were successful because they had influence.

Authority tells people what to do. Influence helps people see why it matters. Authority can create compliance. Influence creates commitment. The difference between the two is not subtle once you have seen it in action. Authority depends on positional power, the formal right to make decisions or set direction. Influence depends on personal power, the ability to earn trust, to communicate meaningfully, and to build relationships that hold under pressure.

Organizations consistently overestimate how far authority will carry them during change. Research from the Edelman Trust Barometer, one of the most comprehensive annual studies of trust across industries and countries, shows year after year that people place significantly greater confidence in someone like them, a peer, a direct colleague, a change leader they know personally, than in a senior executive they rarely interact with. This means that during change, the most influential voices are often closer to the front line than the boardroom. When these individuals believe in a change, their belief spreads. When they doubt it, their doubt spreads even faster.

Think of influence the way you think about a chess board rather than a checkers board. In checkers, every piece moves the same way, and every situation calls for the same response. Push harder when blocked. Advance when clear. In chess, every piece has a different capability, a different range, a different role. Reading the board means understanding not just where the pieces are but how each one moves, what each one is protecting, and what the position will look like three moves from now. Change leaders who develop this kind of situational intelligence stop asking why something is blocked and start asking what is being protected, and how they can work with that rather than against it.

Influence in change leadership moves in three directions - *upwards, lateral and around.*

> **Leading upward** requires clarity and conciseness. Senior stakeholders are influenced by insights that respect their priorities and address their concerns without demanding more of their attention than necessary.
>
> **Leading laterally** requires collaboration and genuine partnership. Peers are not influenced through pressure. They are influenced through shared ownership and mutual respect.
>
> **Leading the people around** you requires transparency, encouragement, and a presence that makes people feel supported rather than managed.

Leading across all three directions requires both adaptive leadership and influence.

Credibility is influence's closest companion, and it grows slowly, through countless interactions that individually seem small but collectively define how others experience you. By keeping commitments, being transparent in difficult moments, being honest when the answer is unclear, and being fair in decisions that carry weight.

During change, credibility becomes even more essential because people are more attuned to every signal a change leader sends. They watch closely to see whether the person asking them to change is willing to change themselves. They notice whether the values being spoken about are the values being lived. Change leaders who protect their credibility protect their influence. Change leaders who compromise their credibility compromise their impact, often in ways they do not fully recover from.

Early in my career, I was part of a team preparing a significant proposal for executive approval. We had spent weeks building the business case. The logic was sound. The data was strong. The strategic alignment was clear. Yet every time we presented it to the leadership team, the conversation stalled. We kept refining the deck, sharpening the argument, adding more evidence. Nothing worked.

When we finally stepped back and looked honestly at the situation, the problem became clear. We had been speaking at the decision makers rather than with them. We had not taken the time to understand what mattered most to each of them individually, what they feared, what pressures they were navigating, what trade-offs they were trying to balance. We focused on the proposal and did not deeply understand our stakeholders' needs. In change leadership, we draw on a principle well established in motivation psychology and adult learning: the **WIIFM** principle, What's In It For Me. It is one of the oldest and most validated truths in human motivation, and one of the most consistently overlooked principles in stakeholder engagement.

We changed our approach. Before going back to the group, we met individually with each executive. Not to sell the idea. To listen. Those conversations revealed something the formal presentations never could. Each leader carried a different unspoken concern. One was worried about timing. Another about capacity. A third about how the change would be perceived by a key external partner. None of these concerns had appeared in the room during our presentations because the room did not feel like a safe place to be uncertain.

By the time we reconvened, the dynamic was different. We came back not with a better argument but with a genuine understanding. The proposal moved forward. But more importantly, the relationships that made that approval possible went on to shape every subsequent conversation that initiative required. That experience changed how I approach influence permanently.

> Influence is not something you wield. It is something you cultivate. It grows through curiosity, humility, and the willingness to understand before you try to be understood.

What that experience also taught me is the difference between declared alignment and discovered alignment. *Declared alignment* happens when a change is announced, and it is assumed everyone is moving together because no one has publicly disagreed. *Discovered alignment* happens when a change leader takes the time to understand what each person believes about the change, what they fear, what they value, and what they need to see before they can genuinely commit. **One creates the appearance of unity. The other creates the reality of it.**

Through my change leadership journey, I have developed a simple practice for distinguishing between the two. Before any significant alignment conversation, I ask myself five questions. I call them the Discovered Alignment Questions, and they have become one of the most reliable tools in my practice.

1. What does each person in this room believe is changing, and do those beliefs match?
2. What is each person most afraid of losing, and has anyone created space for that fear to be named?
3. Where is agreement being performed vs. genuinely held?
4. What would each person need to see, hear, or experience before they could move from intellectual agreement to genuine commitment?
5. And finally: if I removed every person from this room and spoke with them individually, would the conversation sound the same as it does in the group?

If the answer to that last question is no, you do not have alignment. You have declared alignment, the kind that looks like unity in the meeting and quietly unravels in the hallway afterward. Discovered alignment requires the patience to sit with each of these questions long enough to hear what people are not yet saying in the room. It is slower. It is more demanding. And it is the only kind that holds when the change becomes difficult.

This is what Ronald Heifetz, one of the most original thinkers in modern leadership, means when he distinguishes between technical problems and adaptive challenges. Technical problems have known solutions. They can be resolved with expertise, the right process, and the right tools. Adaptive challenges are fundamentally different. They require people to change their beliefs, behaviours, values, and ways of working. They cannot be solved with a better presentation or a clearer mandate. They require a different kind of leadership entirely, one that begins not with the answer but with a genuine understanding of the situation.

Heifetz uses the metaphor of the balcony and the dance floor to describe what adaptive leadership demands. When you are on the dance floor, you are inside the action, engaged with the immediate pressures and personalities around you. You can see what is directly in front of you, but you cannot see the full pattern of the room. The balcony gives you that view. From the balcony you can see who is leading whom, where the energy is flowing, where people are stuck, and what the room is doing rather than what you assumed it was doing. Adaptive leaders move between the dance floor and the balcony. They engage fully with the complexity of the situation while also creating the space to observe it clearly enough to understand what kind of challenge they are facing.

But the balcony alone is not enough. Reading the room from above is only the beginning. What adaptive leadership requires is the ability to read three things simultaneously and then adjust accordingly. *The stakeholder, situation and themselves.*

The first is the stakeholder. Who is this person? What drives them? What do they fear losing? What do they need from this interaction that they may not be saying directly? A senior executive navigating board pressure needs something different from a frontline team member managing workload anxiety. A long-tenured employee whose identity is tied to the way things have always been done needs something different from a newer team member who sees the change as an opportunity. Adaptive change leaders do not treat all stakeholders the same way because they are not all the same. They observe, they listen, and they adjust their approach to meet the person in front of them rather than the person they assumed would be there.

The second is the situation. What is happening beneath the surface of what is being said? Is this a technical problem that needs a clearer process, or an adaptive challenge that needs a different kind of conversation? Is the resistance rooted in a lack of information or a deeper fear about identity and belonging? Is the conflict about the decision itself or about the relationship between the people involved? Adaptive change leaders resist the temptation to diagnose quickly and instead stay curious long enough to understand what kind of challenge they are genuinely facing. Solving an adaptive challenge with a technical tool is one of the most common and costly mistakes in change leadership. It addresses the symptom while the real issue continues to grow.

The third is themselves. What is your default style under pressure? Where do your blind spots live? What does this specific moment require of you that may not come naturally? A change leader who is naturally direct and decisive may need to slow down and listen more in a conversation with a resistant stakeholder. A change leader who is naturally empathetic and patient may need to be more direct when a difficult dynamic requires naming what others are avoiding. Self-awareness, knowing yourself well enough to adjust your approach, without losing your authenticity in the process, is one of the most demanding and most important disciplines in adaptive leadership.

When these three readings come together, the change leader's response becomes genuinely adaptive rather than instinctive. They are not defaulting to their preferred style. They are choosing the approach that the stakeholder, the situation, and the moment require. This is not manipulation. It is intelligence. This means reading the context well enough to behave in the way that serves the people and the change.

The change leader who is direct and data-driven with a finance stakeholder and warm and narrative with a people leader is not being inconsistent. They are being adaptive. The change leader who is direct with senior executives and creates a safe space for questions with anxious frontline teams is not playing two different roles. They are reading the needs of each group and responding accordingly. This is the practical expression of adaptive leadership. Not a framework on a slide. A daily discipline of observation, adjustment, and presence.

Before any significant conversation or work, I run through what I call the Three Reads. It has become one of the most reliable practices in my work.

> **Read the person.** What do I know about this person? What do they likely need from this interaction? What is the history they are carrying into this conversation, and how might it shape what they hear regardless of what I say?

Read the situation. What kind of challenge is this, technical or adaptive? Is the tension about the decision itself, or about the relationship between the people involved? Is there something unspoken that is shaping the dynamic more than anything that has been said?

Read myself. What is my default response likely to be in this situation, and is it the response this moment needs? Where are my blind spots in this conversation? What am I assuming that I should be questioning? And what do I need to let go of, a position, a preference, or a need to be right, to genuinely serve the outcome rather than protect my own comfort?

These three reads do not guarantee a perfect conversation. But they consistently produce a better one. They slow the instinct to react and create space for the discipline of responding. Over time, they become second nature. But in the beginning, writing them down before walking into the room is the most practical thing a change leader can do.

As explored in The Human Side of Change, resistance is not defiance. It is information. It tells change leaders where people are struggling, where trust may be fragile, and where support is most needed. What adaptive leadership adds to that foundation is a practical lens for reading what the resistance is protecting and responding to it with precision rather than pressure.

Sometimes, what is being protected is identity. A technical expert who has built their reputation on mastery of a specific system may resist a new system not because they oppose progress but because they fear becoming less competent. A manager who has led the same team for years may resist structural changes not because they oppose efficiency but because they fear losing the relationships and influence they have spent years building. A long-tenured team member may resist cultural shifts not because they oppose growth but because they fear losing the sense of belonging that has defined their experience of the organization.

Resistance also shows up in ways that are regularly misread. Silence in a meeting is almost never agreement. It is more often self-protection, a decision that speaking up is not safe enough to risk. A barrage of questions is not usually hostility. It is frequently anxiety looking for reassurance. Sarcasm and humour in the face of change almost always signal discomfort that does not yet have permission to be named directly. Delays and missed commitments are not always operational. Sometimes they reflect emotional hesitation that no one has created space to acknowledge. Each of these expressions carries useful information. Change leaders who notice them with sensitivity and respond with curiosity rather than frustration unlock insight that the people sitting quietly in the room are not yet ready to offer directly.

The same principle applies to the organizational politics and hidden dynamics that every change leader eventually encounters. The word "politics" makes most change leaders uncomfortable. Many try to rise above it, to stay neutral, to focus only on the work. But this approach leaves them vulnerable to dynamics they have chosen not to understand. Politics, at its core, is simply the movement of influence through human relationships. Power is neither positive nor negative. It is neutral until shaped by intention. Hidden dynamics are not secrets to be uncovered. They are patterns to be read.

In every organization, decisions are shaped by relationships long before they are shaped by strategy. Conversations happen in hallways and coffee queues long before they happen in formal meetings. People defer to some voices more than others, not always for reasons that appear on any organizational chart. Alliances form around shared interests and shared fears. These dynamics do not represent dysfunction. They represent humanity. People work with those they trust, protect what they value, and resist what feels unsafe or unclear.

Think of organizational politics the way an experienced meteorologist thinks about weather systems. The weather is always present, always moving, and largely invisible until it produces visible effects. You cannot eliminate it. You cannot ignore it without consequences. What you can do is learn to read it early, understand what conditions produce which patterns, and position your change accordingly. Change leaders who develop political intelligence are not playing games. They are becoming skilled readers of the human system they are working within.

David Rock's research through the NeuroLeadership Institute identified five social domains that reliably activate the brain's threat or reward response, which he termed the SCARF model: Status, Certainty, Autonomy, Relatedness, and Fairness. When a change threatens any one of these domains for any individual or group, the threat response activates and resistant or political behaviour almost inevitably follows. A change that reduces someone's perceived status will trigger a status threat. A change that increases uncertainty will trigger a certainty threat. A change that removes choice will trigger an autonomy threat. A change that isolates people from relationships they depend on will trigger a relatedness threat. And a change that feels inconsistent or applied unequally will trigger a fairness threat, often the most emotionally charged of all. Understanding which domain is being threatened in any given situation gives change leaders a practical lens for navigating both resistance and political dynamics rather than simply reacting to them.

Power in organizations is also more fluid and more distributed than formal structures suggest. Some people carry influence through expertise, others through reputation, others through the trust they have built over years of steady integrity. Real power shifts as circumstances change. Change leaders who observe where influence sits, who people turn to when they are uncertain, whose opinion shapes the room before anyone has formally spoken, develop a map of the organization that serves them far better than any reporting structure.

Navigating this landscape requires engaging with it consciously and with grounded integrity rather than either avoiding it or reacting to it. Change leaders who engage with politics ethically do not shy away from power. They understand it well enough to move within it without losing themselves. They know when to listen and when to speak. They know how to build alliances rooted in genuine trust rather than convenience. They know how to address tensions others are ignoring without unnecessarily escalating them. And they know that wherever psychological safety exists, the need for political manoeuvring diminishes because people feel safe enough to say what is true.

All of this, the influence, the adaptive reading of situations, the navigation of resistance and political dynamics, ultimately points toward the same destination: shaping how change leaders think about the difficult stakeholders and challenging dynamics they encounter.

The most powerful shift a change leader can make is moving from trying to convince people to trying to understand them. Difficult stakeholders almost always become partners when engaged with genuine respect and curiosity. The conversation changes entirely when you stop saying we need you to support this and start saying we need your insight to make this stronger. That shift is not a communication technique. It is a fundamental reorientation of the relationship, from one where the change leader holds the answer and needs buy-in, to one where the change leader and the stakeholder build the answer together.

> People support what they help to create. They resist what feels imposed.

This is one of the most enduring principles in change leadership, rooted in Kurt Lewin's foundational research on participative change. This is not a weakness in human nature. It is one of the most reliable truths about how human beings relate to change. The change leaders who understand this stop fighting it and start working with it. They create more opportunities for people to shape what is being built. They ask for perspective before announcing decisions. They invite critical voices into the room rather than managing them from outside it. They treat the most challenging person in the room not as the obstacle to progress but as the person most likely to carry the truth that the change most needs to hear.

Every difficult stakeholder holds something valuable. A risk the team has not considered. A piece of organizational history that explains why a similar approach has failed before. A perspective from the front line that strategy never reaches. A fear that, once named and addressed, removes the last barrier to genuine commitment. Change leaders who understand this do not dread difficult stakeholders. They seek them out.

Influence, adaptive leadership, and navigating hidden dynamics are not skills you acquire and then possess. They are practices you develop through every difficult conversation you choose to stay present in, every piece of resistance you choose to understand rather than overcome, every power dynamic you choose to name rather than navigate around. They deepen with each change you lead, each relationship you invest in, and each moment you choose curiosity over judgment.

The change leaders who move organizations forward are not always the ones with the most authority. They are the ones people trust enough to follow through in uncertainty. And that trust is built not in grand moments but in the quiet, consistent, courageous choices made one conversation at a time.

John C. Maxwell captured this truth in seven words: **Leadership is influence. Nothing more. Nothing less.**

In change leadership, how you adapt is how you influence.

YOUR CHANGE LEADER JOURNAL

One Key Takeaway What insight about influence, adaptive leadership, or navigating hidden dynamics resonated most deeply with me?

What Might Hold Me Back What beliefs, habits, or fears might limit my ability to influence without authority or navigate resistance with curiosity?

The Action I Am Committed to Taking Which relationship will I intentionally invest in, and what will I do differently in that relationship?

One Simple Step I Can Take Today Identify one person whose resistance or behaviour I have been frustrated by, and ask myself: what might this be protecting?

07

Communication That Moves the Needle

"The single biggest problem in communication is the illusion that it has taken place."

George Bernard Shaw

It is March 23, 2020. New Zealand has just recently confirmed its first case of community transmission of COVID-19. Jacinda Ardern, the country's Prime Minister, is about to communicate to a nation that is frightened, uncertain, and watching leaders around the world respond with varying degrees of clarity, authority, and humanity. Some are holding formal press conferences behind podiums, surrounded by advisors, reading carefully prepared statements. Some are projecting confidence they do not have. Some are hedging. Some are deflecting.

Ardern makes a different choice.

She goes live on Facebook from her home. No podium. No formal backdrop. No communications team visible behind the camera. She is sitting in what appears to be her living room, in a casual sweater, looking directly into the lens as if she is talking to a friend rather than addressing a nation. She does not begin with statistics or policy timelines. She begins with acknowledgment. She names the fear people are feeling. She explains the logic of the lockdown in plain, unhurried language. She says *we* and *together* and *I know this is hard* in ways that feel unrehearsed because they are. When people begin sending questions in real time, she answers them. Not the easy ones. The hard ones. The ones about job security, childcare, and whether elderly parents will be safe.

Within days, New Zealand's compliance with lockdown measures becomes among the highest recorded anywhere in the world during the pandemic. Researchers who later studied the response pointed not to the policy itself as the primary driver of that compliance, but to the communication. The result was measurable: New Zealand recorded one of the lowest per-capita COVID mortality rates in the developed world in 2020, and its economy was among the first to recover. People trusted her. Not because she was authoritative, though she was. Not because she had all the answers, because she did not. But because she had chosen to be human in a moment when humanity was what people needed most.

She had not simply informed a nation. She had moved it. That distinction, between informing people and moving them, is what this chapter is about.

In every change I have witnessed, communication has been the thread that either holds people together or quietly unravels the fabric of trust. It is easy to think of communication as a function, something to distribute, to cascade, to deliver. But communication is not a task. It is a relationship. And during change, it becomes the relationship people depend on most. Yet most organizations approach change communication the way they approach corporate communications. Announce it. Cascade it. Repeat it. Measure reach and open rates and call it done. Send the email. Run the town hall. Publish the FAQ. Tick the box marked "communicated."

George Bernard Shaw understood this well. The illusion that communication has taken place is one of the most expensive mistakes an organization can make during change. You can fill every inbox, hold every all-hands meeting, and publish every update on every channel available to you, and still have a workforce that does not know why the change is happening, does not believe what they are being told, and does not feel safe enough to ask the questions that are keeping them up at night.

This is because corporate communication and change communication are not the same discipline. They are not asking the same question.

> **Corporate communication asks:** Did people receive the message?
>
> **Change communication asks:** Did the message change anything?

One measures distribution. The other measures shift. Corporate communication is designed to inform. Change communication is designed to move, to shift beliefs, behaviours, and emotional states in ways that make change not only understood but genuinely embraced. Treating these as interchangeable is one of the most common and most costly mistakes in change leadership. It produces organizations full of people who have technically been told everything and emotionally received nothing.

Let me make this concrete. Imagine an organization announcing a restructuring. Here is what corporate communication typically produces:

> "Following a strategic review, we are realigning our organizational structure to better position us for future growth. These changes will take effect over the coming months. Further information will be shared in due course. We remain committed to supporting all employees through this transition."

Every sentence is technically accurate. Not one of them is useful to the person reading it at 9:14 am on a Tuesday morning, heart rate elevated, wondering whether they still have a role.

Here is what change communication sounds like:

> "We are making changes to how our teams are structured. Some roles will change. Some will be new. I want to be honest with you: not every decision has been finalized, and I know that uncertainty is uncomfortable. Here is what I can tell you today. Here is what is still being decided. Here is when you will hear more. And here is how you can ask questions or raise concerns in the meantime. You will not be left without information, and you will not be left without support."

The difference is not polish. It is orientation. The first message was generic language written for the organization. The second was written for the person reading it. That is the distinction between corporate communication and change communication, and it is the distinction that determines whether people lean in or shut down.

Neuroscience helps explain why. Research on how the brain processes information during change suggests that emotional responses tend to precede deliberative thinking. **People do not first absorb facts during change. They first absorb feeling.** They listen for reassurance before they listen for information. They listen for safety before they listen for strategy. They ask, consciously or not, can I trust this person before they ask what this person is saying. A perfectly crafted message delivered without emotional intelligence will still fail to land because the receiver's nervous system has already decided whether to let it in.

This is why an email with perfect grammar and bulletproof logic can leave people more anxious than they were before they read it. And why a simple, transparent, humanly delivered message from a leader people trust can restore calm even when the road ahead is genuinely unclear.

People are not resistant to information. They are resistant to feeling unseen, dismissed, or emotionally abandoned in the middle of uncertainty.

And beneath every professional question people ask during change, there is almost always a more personal one they are not asking out loud:

> *Will I be okay? Will I belong here when this is done? Do they know what this means for my workload? Is leadership being honest with us? Do they see how tired we already are? Is everything I rely on about to change?*

These are not operational questions. They are existential ones. They speak to identity, stability, safety, and meaning. When change leaders communicate only to the operational question and ignore the existential one, their messages land in the wrong place entirely. They address the mind and miss the person.

Before a change leader communicates anything, they need to understand their audience. Not their title or their department. Their reality. What pressures are they currently carrying? How much change have they already absorbed? What do they fear most about this specific change? And what do they most need to hear right now, not what the organization needs to say, but what that specific person needs to receive?

This is the WIIFM principle in communication. You will recall from Chapter 6 that What's In It For Me is one of the oldest and most validated truths in human motivation. Nowhere does it apply more directly than in how change leaders communicate. Every stakeholder is listening to every message through the filter of what does this mean for me. The change leader who understands this stops broadcasting and starts translating.

Translation is the real skill of change communication. A skilled translator does not simply convert words from one language to another. They convert meaning. The same sentence in two different languages does not just use different words. It carries different cultural weight, different connotations, and different emotional resonance. A translator who only converts words produces something technically accurate but humanly foreign. A translator who converts meaning produces something that lands.

Change communication works exactly this way. The change leader's job is not to broadcast the message in the language of the strategy. It is to translate that message into the language of the person receiving it. The senior finance leader needs it in the language of risk and return. The frontline team member needs it in the language of what changes on Monday morning. The long-tenured employee needs it in the language of what will stay the same. The anxious middle manager needs it in the language of what support is available and who to call when things get hard.

Same message. Different translations. All of them honest. All of them necessary. This is not manipulation. It is communication intelligence.

Data is one of the most powerful tools available to a change leader, but only when it is used to tell a story rather than present evidence. Evidence requires the receiver to do the interpretive work. A story does that work for them. Consider the difference between these two statements.

> 80% of our people say they do not understand why this change is happening. And: eight out of every ten people on your team walked in this morning without knowing why their work is about to change.

The number is identical. The emotional landing is completely different. One invites analysis. The other invites action.

Understanding your audience shapes how you use data. Some people are *Head* communicators. They process through logic, numbers, and evidence. They want data presented with precision, connected to outcomes they are accountable for, and free of emotional framing that feels like it is managing them rather than informing them. Other people are *Heart* communicators. They process through narrative and human impact. They want to understand what the numbers mean for real people in real situations. Presenting raw data to a Heart communicator without translating it into human terms is like handing someone a map in a language they cannot read.

> The most effective change communicators know which room they are in before they decide how to speak in it.

There are four misconceptions about communication that change leaders encounter repeatedly, and each quietly undermines well-designed change efforts.

The **first** is that more communication equals better communication. It does not. More poorly targeted, poorly timed, or poorly translated communication does not build clarity. It builds noise. And noise increases anxiety rather than reducing it. More is not better. Better is better.

The **second** is that clear messaging equals understanding. It does not. A perfectly clear message can still fail to land because the receiver's emotional state, their history with the organization, their current level of trust in leadership, and the competing information they are processing simultaneously all shape what they hear. The telephone wire between sender and receiver is never a perfect conductor. There is always interference. The conditions of the line, the emotional climate of the organization, the noise of competing priorities, and the weight of past experiences all affect what gets through. Change leaders who assume the message was received as intended are making the most dangerous assumption in change leadership. The question is never only what was said. It is always what did they hear.

The **third** is that corporate communication and change communication are the same discipline. They are not, and treating them as interchangeable is one of the costliest mistakes organizations make during change. Corporate communication is built for reach. Change communication is built for shift. One measures whether people received the message. The other measures whether anything changed because of it.

The **fourth** is that communication is primarily about speaking and sharing information. It is not. The most powerful communication tool a change leader possesses is listening. Not performative listening while waiting for a turn to speak, but listening, with the kind of attention that makes the other person feel genuinely heard rather than professionally managed.

I want to share a story about a moment that reframed how I think about communication in change leadership. I was supporting a senior leader who was preparing to announce a significant restructuring to their team. The communications team had spent two weeks developing the message. It had been reviewed, refined, and approved at every level. It was comprehensive, professionally worded, and strategically sound. But when the leader rehearsed it before the announcement, it fell flat.

Because the script was not theirs. They were performing a message rather than delivering one. And people, who are extraordinarily attuned to the difference between authenticity and performance, would feel it the moment the leader began to speak.

I asked the leader a simple question. How do you feel about this announcement?

They put the script down. And what came out over the next few minutes was something the communications team had never captured. They described the weight of the decision. The weeks of debate before the final call was made. The genuine care they felt for the people whose roles were changing. The fact that they had lost sleep over it. And the commitment they were making, personally, to support every person through the transition. None of that was in the script.

They also named something quieter but equally real: the fear of appearing vulnerable in front of their team, of showing uncertainty in a moment when people were looking to them for strength.

We rebuilt the script together from what they had just shared. The following day, the leader faced their team and spoke from that place instead. They acknowledged the difficulty of the decision and expressed genuine gratitude for what their team had built. They named the uncertainty honestly rather than smoothing over it. Then they made specific commitments: what would happen next, how people would be supported, and a promise to remain present and transparent throughout, even without all the answers.

The room did not erupt in celebration. But it held. People listened with their defences down rather than up. Several came forward afterward to say they appreciated the honesty. The message was still difficult. But it was human. And humanity, in that moment, was what the room needed most.

A change leader's presence communicates before their words do. Tone, timing, eye contact, posture, the degree of stillness or restlessness in the body, all of these send messages that arrive before the first sentence is spoken. Change leaders who understand this do not simply prepare what to say. They prepare how they show up, and how they help the people they support show up.

Clarity is a form of respect. When change leaders speak in corporate language, in optimizations and realignments and strategic pivots, they are not protecting anyone. They are creating distance. They are signalling that the real conversation is happening somewhere else, in a room the audience is not invited into. People read that signal clearly, even when they cannot name it. And what it communicates is not sophistication. It is evasion.

People deserve directness. They can handle difficult news far better than they can handle the sense that they are being managed rather than trusted. The six things people most need to understand during change are: *why this is happening, what it means for the people around them, what specifically is changing, what is staying the same, what decisions are still being made, and how they will be supported through it.*

A change leader who can help answer these six questions clearly, honestly, and in plain language has done more for their change than any communication plan ever written.

Communication is not a one-time event. It is a rhythm. And the right rhythm is not determined by how much there is to say but by what people need to hear at each stage of the journey. The right message, delivered to the right audience, through the right channel, at the right moment, with the right frequency for that specific context, is what effective change communication looks like.

This means sometimes communicating less than you think you should. It means resisting the temptation to fill silence with noise. It means trusting that a short, honest, well-timed message will do more than a long, comprehensive one that arrives at the wrong moment or in the wrong register for the room receiving it.

People do not need certainty from change leaders. They need transparency and presence. "Here is what we know, here is what we do not know yet, and here is what we are doing next" is more reassuring than any perfectly crafted message that pretends the path is clearer than it is. Consistency that is maintained not just in formal communications but in every hallway conversation, every team meeting, and every moment where the opportunity arises, is what builds the kind of communication credibility that carries people through the hardest parts of any change.

Research by Jack Zenger and Joseph Folkman, published in Harvard Business Review, found that the best listeners are not simply skilled at remaining silent while others speak. They ask questions that open thinking rather than close it. They make connections between what is being said and what is not. John C. Maxwell dedicated an entire book to this practice, *titled Good Leaders Ask Great Questions*. The principle is simple but profound. Change leaders who ask the right question at the right moment create something more valuable than information. They create connection. They make people feel genuinely heard rather than simply listened to, and that distinction matters more than most communicators realize.

I experienced this firsthand during a session I was facilitating with a team that had been navigating back-to-back changes for months. I had a detailed agenda prepared. Structured exercises. Clear outcomes. But when I walked into the room, I could feel the weight in the air. It was the heaviness of people who have been asked to keep moving without anyone acknowledging how far they have already come. I closed my laptop. I stepped forward.

And I said, let's put the agenda aside for a moment. What is on people's minds today?

There was silence. Then one voice spoke. *I am tired.*

Then another. *I feel like we are navigating this without a map.*

Then another. *I worry we are not being told everything.*

The room opened. The agenda disappeared. We spent most of the session simply listening to each other. And when we eventually returned to the work, something fundamental had shifted. People were not just present in the room. They were present with each other. The communication that happened in that unscripted hour accomplished more than any structured session could have, because it created the one condition that makes all other communication possible: the feeling that it is safe to say what is true.

In Part I of this book, you explored the anatomy of a change leader through the Head, the Heart, and the Hands. Those same three dimensions shape how communication either moves people or fails to reach them.

Communication that moves the needle is not a technique or a skill set. It operates on three levels simultaneously. At the level of the Head, it offers clarity, vision, rationale, and honest answers to the six questions people need answered before they can begin to move. At the level of the Heart, it creates safety, the emotional assurance that people are seen, that their experience matters, and that they are not navigating this alone. And at the level of the Hands, it creates movement, the specific, practical next steps that turn understanding into action and intention into progress.

Most change leaders naturally gravitate toward one dimension. Some lead heavily from the Head. Some remember the Hands. And some lead consistently with the Heart. All three are important, and the most effective change leaders and communicators adapt across all of them depending on the audience, the moment, and what the change requires. The Heart is the gateway through which the Head and the Hands become possible. Without emotional safety, clarity becomes information overload, and action becomes compliance. With it, clarity becomes orientation and action becomes commitment.

The change leaders who communicate in ways that move the needle are not necessarily the most polished speakers or the most prolific communicators. They are the ones who understand that communication is ultimately an act of service. It exists not to transmit what the change leader needs to say but to create what the people receiving it need to feel, think, and do. When change leaders hold that distinction at the centre of every communication decision they make, the needle moves.

Not because people were told what to do. Because they felt understood well enough to choose it themselves.

YOUR CHANGE LEADER JOURNAL

One Key Takeaway What insight about communication shifted my understanding of how people experience change?

What Might Hold Me Back What personal habits, assumptions, or fears might prevent me from communicating with clarity and humanity?

The Action I Am Committed to Taking What intentional communication will I deliver this week to build trust and connection with my team or stakeholders?

One Simple Step I Can Take Today Ask one person: 'What would help you feel more supported or informed right now?' Then listen without defence.

08

Leading and Sustaining Momentum Through the Middle

"It does not matter how slowly you go as long as you do not stop."

Confucius

Momentum is one of the most powerful forces in any change. It is the quiet current that carries people forward, the sense of movement that reassures them that progress is possible, and the energy that turns intention into reality.

In 1914, Ernest Shackleton set out to lead the first land crossing of the Antarctic continent. It was one of the most ambitious expeditions in human history. He recruited 27 men, assembled a ship called the Endurance, and sailed toward a destination that most people who attempted it did not survive.

The expedition never reached its goal. In January 1915, before the team could even begin the land crossing, the Endurance became trapped in pack ice in the Weddell Sea. Then it began to break apart. Over the following months, Shackleton watched his ship, his plan, and his original purpose be slowly crushed by forces entirely beyond his control.

What happened next is one of the most extraordinarily sustained leadership performances in recorded history.

For nearly two years, Shackleton kept 27 men alive, engaged, and moving forward in conditions of extreme cold, total isolation, dwindling supplies, and zero certainty of survival. They camped on the ice as the ship sank beneath them. They dragged lifeboats across frozen terrain. They endured months of darkness in the Antarctic winter. They faced frostbite, hunger, exhaustion, and the psychological weight of not knowing whether anyone in the world even knew they were still alive. The odds of survival were, by any rational calculation, not in their favour.

What Shackleton understood, intuitively and with extraordinary discipline, was that momentum in those conditions had nothing to do with speed or progress toward the original destination. It had everything to do with his people's sustained belief that the journey was worth continuing. He created structure in chaos, small rituals that gave each day shape and meaning. He assigned roles that gave every person a sense of contribution. He celebrated small wins with genuine enthusiasm, a good meal found in the supplies, a navigational milestone reached, and a day of better weather. He regulated the emotional climate of the camp with conscious intention, staying calm when others panicked, expressing confidence without false certainty, and acknowledging difficulty without amplifying fear. He understood that his most important job was not to get his team to the destination. It was to keep them believing the destination existed.

When Shackleton finally reached South Georgia Island after an 800-mile open-ocean crossing in a lifeboat, and mounted a rescue mission that returned every single member of his crew alive, historians did not credit the outcome to luck or heroism alone. They credited it to the sustained quality of his leadership through the exhausting, uncertain, belief-testing middle of an experience that had every reason to collapse into despair.

There is something in the Shackleton story that is easily missed, and it speaks directly to the theme of this chapter.

What Shackleton demonstrated was not simply the ability to sustain morale. It was the ability to continuously redefine what "forward" meant as the original definition became impossible.

The expedition set out to cross the Antarctic continent. When the ship was trapped, forward was no longer the continent. It became survival on the ice. When the ice began breaking, forward became reaching Elephant Island. When Elephant Island offered no rescue, forward became the 800-mile crossing to South Georgia. At every stage, the definition of progress changed entirely. And at every stage, Shackleton had to do something that most leadership accounts gloss over: he had to grieve the previous definition of success, privately and without burdening his team with that grief, before he could credibly cast the next one.

> This is the precise challenge that change leaders face in the sustained middle of any change. The original vision may need to be revised. The timeline may need to shift. The scope may need to contract or expand.

And each of those revisions requires the change leader to release what was promised and redefine what forward looks like now, without allowing that redefinition to feel like failure to the people who are already tired.

Shackleton's genius was not that he kept people moving. It was that he kept redefining the destination in ways that preserved belief. That is the most demanding and least discussed skill of leading through the middle.

That middle is where most change initiatives either hold or fall apart. Not at the beginning, when energy is high and the vision is fresh. Not at the end, when the finish line is visible and momentum carries itself. In the middle, when the initial excitement has faded, the destination feels distant, fatigue has accumulated, and people are quietly asking themselves whether the effort is still worth sustaining.

This chapter is about the middle. About what it takes to keep a change moving when the conditions are not in your favour, when people are tired, when the purpose needs to be rediscovered, and when the most important thing a change leader can do is tend the flame rather than push the pace. Today's change leaders may not face 22 months on the Antarctic ice, but the speed of change brings its own version of uncertainty, disruption, and exhaustion. The terrain is different. The human challenge at the centre of it has not changed.

When momentum is present, people lean in. They stay engaged. They begin to believe that the change is not just an idea but something real that is unfolding around them. But momentum, like fire, does not sustain itself. It must be tended.

Think of momentum as a campfire. It does not maintain itself once it is lit. It requires tending. Someone must add fuel at the right moments, protect the flame from the wind, and rebuild when the fire begins to die down. Change leaders who understand this do not assume momentum will maintain itself once established. They watch for when the energy is dropping before it drops completely. They add small wins, recognition, and moments of acknowledgement the way a campfire needs smaller pieces of wood before the larger ones. Because momentum, like fire, is far easier to sustain than to restart once it has gone out.

In my experience, momentum does not collapse suddenly. It erodes. And by the time a change leader recognizes that momentum has been lost, they are already dealing with a recovery rather than a prevention. I have learned to watch for five early signals that tell me momentum is beginning to thin before it becomes visible to anyone else.

The first signal is a language shift. When people begin describing the change as something happening to them rather than something they are part of, ownership is quietly transferring away from the team and back to the project. Listen for the shift in language. It tells you more than any status report.

The second is meeting energy. When the opening minutes of a meeting carry a different weight than they did a month ago, when people arrive later, contribute less, or default to updates rather than problem-solving, the collective energy is dropping.

The third is decision avoidance. When decisions that should be straightforward begin taking longer, when people defer to others or request more data before committing, the confidence that underpins momentum is weakening.

The fourth is silence from advocates. Every change has early supporters who carry the message into rooms the project team cannot reach. When those voices go quiet, it is often because they no longer feel confident in what they are advocating for. Their silence is a leading indicator.

The fifth is nostalgia. When people begin referencing how things used to be done with warmth or longing, particularly in casual conversation rather than formal settings, they are signalling that the emotional cost of the change is beginning to outweigh the perceived benefit.

Each of these signals is an invitation to act before the fire goes out. Not with more pressure. With more presence, more acknowledgment, and more visible evidence that the journey is still moving and still worth sustaining.

You will recall from Chapter 3 that Teresa Amabile and Steven Kramer's research on the progress principle showed that even small visible progress is one of the strongest drivers of motivation and engagement. That principle applies here in the sustained middle of a change, when the initial excitement has faded and the destination still feels distant. It is precisely here that when progress feels hardest to see, making it visible matters most.

> People do not need perfection to keep going. They need to feel that the journey is moving and that their effort is producing something real.

Momentum matters because humans are deeply influenced by the perception of progress. Not massive progress. Consistent progress. Each small step forward reinforces belief that the goal is achievable and that the effort is worth sustaining. When progress goes unseen, energy depletes. When progress is acknowledged, even quietly, energy renews.

I was brought into an organization that had been trying to move a change forward for longer than anyone was comfortable admitting. From the outside, it looked like a resistance and readiness problem. From a leadership perspective, the diagnosis was clear: the staff were not on board. That was why they brought me in. Not to examine the change itself or the leadership approach around it. To get the people moving.

When I began speaking with staff before the session, a different picture emerged. People were not resistant. They were fatigued. They were silent. There is an important difference. Resistance is active. Silence is self-protection. These were people who had learned, through experience, that voicing what they thought about the change carried a cost they were not willing to pay. So, they did what people do in those conditions. They showed up. They complied. They gave leadership what they believed leadership wanted. And nothing moved.

During the session, I created anonymous real-time feedback loops, structured ways for people to share what they were genuinely experiencing without their names attached to their honesty. What came back was not complaints or grievances. It was clarity. People knew exactly what was getting in the way. They had simply never been given a safe place to say it.

When these insights began to surface, something happened that I have seen before but never stops being instructive. Leadership responded defensively. Not maliciously. Not even consciously. But the posture, the tone, the instinct to explain and justify rather than listen, was immediate. And in that moment, without anyone having to name it, the room understood something important. The dynamic the staff had described in their anonymous feedback was unfolding in real time, right in front of everyone.

I did not point to it directly. I did not need to. I simply slowed the conversation down and created space for leaders to hear themselves. To notice what their responses were communicating. To sit with the discomfort of recognizing something true about themselves rather than rushing past it.

Good leaders, when given the genuine opportunity to see themselves clearly, almost always choose to look.

By the afternoon, we moved into something different entirely. A trust-building session with a physical obstacle course, where participants had to guide and support each other through navigating challenges they could not complete alone. They had to communicate in real time. Support each other through uncertainty. Trust that the person beside them would lead them in the right direction.

What the obstacle course did was make the morning conversation be felt rather than just understood. You can hear that trust requires vulnerability. You can agree with it intellectually. But when you are standing at an obstacle and the only way through is to lean on someone you have not yet fully trusted, the understanding becomes embodied. It becomes real.

By the end of the day, the atmosphere in the room had shifted in a way that no strategy session had managed to produce. Not because anyone had been convinced of anything. Because people had experienced something together that words alone could not have created. The change did not resolve itself that afternoon. But it began to move. And in the life of a stalled change, movement is everything. Alignment is not created by announcing a direction. It is discovered by building a shared meaning. Shared meaning is what helps the change move forward with aligned momentum.

Every change follows an emotional curve. It begins with anticipation or curiosity, rises briefly with possibility, and then dips as reality sets in. People encounter unexpected challenges, experience fatigue, and begin to question whether the pace or the direction is right. This dip is not a sign that something has gone wrong. It is a natural part of the change journey.

Change leaders who understand this curve are more patient and more compassionate during the difficult middle. They anticipate these emotional shifts and respond in ways that keep people grounded rather than overwhelmed.

What makes the middle of change so hard is not the work itself. It is the presence of uncertainty, the erosion of trust when communication breaks down, and the absence of visible progress combined with the presence of continued demand. Especially in today's world where people are being asked to adapt without being given the space to recover. This is the breeding ground for change fatigue, and it is one of the most underacknowledged challenges in change leadership.

Change fatigue is not lack of resilience. It is the accumulated weight of sustained adaptation without adequate recovery. It is the emotional and cognitive exhaustion that accumulates when people are repeatedly asked to adapt without the time or support to recover. Research consistently identifies change fatigue as one of the top contributors to change failure across industries. Resilience, as Martin Seligman's decades of research confirm, is not a fixed trait. It is cultivated. And change leaders are the ones who help cultivate it.

Change fatigue shows up in ways that are easily misread. Low emotional energy in meetings. Reduced engagement from people. Unanswered emails. Absence from meetings. An increase in cynicism that comes across as negativity or pushback. Delayed decisions. Each of these is a signal, and the appropriate response is never more pressure.

When change fatigue sets in, the most powerful thing a change leader can do is stop pushing harder and start creating the conditions for people to find their strength again. This requires attending to three things simultaneously.

The first is capability. People cannot sustain momentum if they feel unprepared for what the change requires of them. Change fatigue deepens when people are not only tired but uncertain about whether they have what it takes to succeed in the new environment. Change leaders address this by empowering others, providing clarity about what is expected, offering the support and development people need to build confidence, and creating enough psychological safety for people to admit when they feel out of their depth without fear of judgment. As Amy Edmondson's research on psychological safety reminds us, teams that feel safe to speak honestly are more adaptive, more creative, and more resilient under pressure.

The second is participation. People sustain momentum when they feel that they are shaping the change rather than being shaped by it. When people are invited into decisions, asked for their perspectives, and given opportunities to influence the direction, their relationship to the change shifts. They stop seeing themselves as passengers and start seeing themselves as co-creators. That shift is one of the most powerful momentum levers available to a change leader. You will recall from Chapter 6 that people support what they help to create and resist what feels imposed. Nowhere is this more practically important than in the sustained middle of a change when people need a reason to stay engaged. This is collaboration.

The third is emotional support. People need to feel that the change leader sees them as human beings, not just as resources in a project plan. Emotional support does not mean shielding people from difficulty. It means acknowledging the difficulty honestly and offering compassion and steadiness as people navigate it. It means creating space for an honest conversation rather than the performance of resilience. It means leading with empathy and emotional intelligence.

Change leaders who attend to all three dimensions, *capability, participation, and emotional support*, create the conditions in which people find within themselves the energy to keep going. This is resilience in its truest sense. Not a motivational speech. Not a recognition award. The daily, deliberate act of making people feel capable, included, and seen.

One of the most common and least discussed reasons momentum stalls in the middle of a change is not fatigue alone. It is misalignment around purpose. This is why sustaining momentum is not simply a matter of maintaining pace. It is a matter of continuously returning people to the why.

Purpose is the fuel that keeps the fire burning when the initial excitement has faded and the work becomes demanding. Change leaders who make it a practice to reconnect people to meaning, not only at the beginning of a change but throughout its entire arc, create a different quality of engagement than those who treat purpose as an episodic launch event and move on.

> Change leadership is not a sprint. It is more like a trail run through changing terrain, where conditions shift without warning, the path is not always clear, and the most important skill is not speed but the ability to adapt your pace to what the ground beneath you demands.

Marathon runners understand something that sprinters do not. Pacing is not weakness. It is strategy. The runner who goes out too fast in the first miles does not finish strong. The runner who builds in recovery, who knows when to push and when to conserve, who takes water at every station without shame, is the one who crosses the finish line with something left. Change leaders who understand pacing create sustainable momentum. They do not ask their people to push indefinitely. They build in recovery, celebrate the miles already covered, and adjust the pace when the terrain demands it. This is not slowing down. It is leading for the long gain.

Pacing and making progress visible are two of the simplest and most powerful momentum practices available to a change leader. Progress often happens in slow, steady increments that go unnoticed precisely because they are not dramatic enough to announce. A process that has been piloted. A relational barrier that has softened. A decision-making bottleneck that has been resolved. A new collaboration pattern between two teams that had barely spoken before. These are the small but significant movements that collectively constitute real change.

Each of these is a small win. And small wins, named and acknowledged, are what keep a change moving when the larger destination is still out of sight. This is the change leader's responsibility. Not only to drive the change forward but to help people see what progress looks like while they are still inside it.

Sustaining momentum is not optional during change. It is a requirement throughout it. It does not require grand gestures or dedicated off-sites. It requires more than pace and visible progress. It requires consistently and intentionally tending to the energy and belief of the people doing the work, not just at the beginning or end, but throughout every difficult stretch in between.

Change leaders who sustain momentum and model steadiness during the difficult middle create an emotional climate where people feel safe enough to keep going. When change leaders remain grounded, people feel grounded. When change leaders acknowledge fatigue without collapsing into it, people feel permission to acknowledge their own. And when change leaders demonstrate through their own behaviour that it is possible to keep going with grace rather than force, people find that possibility within themselves.

Shackleton never crossed the Antarctic continent. The expedition he set out to lead did not achieve its original goal. By any conventional measure of project success, the Endurance expedition failed. And yet it is studied, taught, and referenced more than almost any other leadership story of the twentieth century. Not because of what Shackleton achieved. Because of how he led when the original plan was gone, the conditions were hostile, and the only thing left to navigate by was his people's sustained belief that they would find their way through.

That is the kind of momentum this chapter is about. Not the momentum of a change without disruption or difficulty. But the human-centred momentum of a change led in a way that the people going through it will remember not for what it cost them, but for how they were led through it.

The change leaders who understand this do not measure their success only by whether the change reached its destination. They measure it by whether the people they led through it arrived intact, still believing, still capable, and still willing to take the next step.

Tend the fire. Make the progress visible. Return people to purpose. The change will keep moving, not because people were pushed, but because they chose to keep going.

YOUR CHANGE LEADER JOURNAL

One Key Takeaway What insight about momentum, fatigue, or resilience resonated most deeply with me?

What Might Hold Me Back What habits or assumptions might make it difficult for me to make space for people to pace and sustain their energy?

The Action I Am Committed to Taking What one act of acknowledgment or support I can offer to my team or stakeholders?

One Simple Step I Can Take Today I will ask one person: "What progress have we made that we have not yet acknowledged?" Then listen with genuine curiosity.

09

Leading Across Teams, Functions, and Culture

"If you want to go fast, go alone.
If you want to go far, go together."
African proverb

Culture is the silent force that shapes how people respond to change. It determines how teams think, communicate, and navigate uncertainty. Culture is not defined by slogans on walls or values written in handbooks. It is defined by daily behaviour. It is defined by what is rewarded, tolerated, repeated, and quietly reinforced. It is defined by the emotional experience people have when they show up to work each day.

A change-ready culture is not created through a single workshop or initiative. It is cultivated through the consistent choices made at every level of the change, and the environment those choices collectively create over time. In a change-ready culture, people do not fear change or disruption. They feel equipped to face it and agile enough to move with it. They do not cling to the past. They honour it while making room for what is emerging. They do not wait for permission to adapt. They step forward because adaptability feels natural.

Think of a change-ready culture the way you think about a garden or healthy ecosystem. Every element, soil, water, light, and living organisms, exists in relationship with every other element. Neglect one, and the others suffer. Add something new, and the whole system adjusts. Culture works the same way. Change one behaviour, and it ripples through the entire environment. A culture becomes change-ready not through a single intervention but through the accumulated health of all its relationships, norms, and daily interactions. Tend to it and you cultivate something more powerful than any strategy: a culture that moves with change rather than against it.

Edgar Schein, one of the most respected organizational culture researchers of the twentieth century, defined culture as the accumulated shared learning of a group. That definition matters for change leaders because it frames culture not as a fixed entity handed down from leadership but as a living accumulation of shared experience. Culture is not what organizations declare. It is what people learn, together, over time, about how things are done. And it is that learned reality, not the stated values, that determines how people respond when change arrives.

There is a common misconception that change readiness is built solely through skills training, communication, or process improvements. While these elements matter, they are not what ultimately determine how people behave. Culture lives deeper. It shapes instinctive reactions and emotional patterns. It shapes how people interpret uncertainty, engage with new ideas, and respond when things become challenging.

A change-ready culture embodies certain qualities: curiosity, openness, humility, empathy, agility, and a shared sense of accountability. These qualities do not eliminate fear or resistance, but they make it possible to navigate them with honesty and courage.

In cultures centred on fear or perfectionism, people avoid risks, hide mistakes, and resist ambiguity. Even the most compelling strategies falter in these environments. In contrast, cultures rooted in psychological safety and learning allow people to adapt naturally. As Google's internal research project, Project Aristotle, found independently, teams with high psychological safety outperform others not because they avoid conflict but because they navigate it productively. A finding that aligned with what Harvard researcher Amy Edmondson had established in her academic research years earlier. They speak honestly. They learn from mistakes. They take risks. They innovate. That capacity does not arrive with people. It is cultivated in the environment that everyone involved in the change helps create.

Satya Nadella understood this when he described what Microsoft needed most not as a new strategy but as a new mindset. The shift he called for, from a know-it-all culture to a learn-it-all culture, transformed one of the world's largest organizations. It was not a restructuring that changed Microsoft. It was a change in what the culture rewarded and what it punished. When learning became more valued than knowing, people began to behave differently. And when people behave differently, the organization becomes capable of different things.

Every team has an emotional climate, even when it is not spoken aloud. This climate influences whether people feel energized or exhausted, whether they lean into new challenges or retreat into old habits. In a change-ready culture, the emotional climate is anchored in trust. People feel valued and respected. They believe their contributions matter. They believe their leaders see them not simply as resources but as human beings with perspectives that add meaning to the work.

In these environments, people ask questions without fear of judgment. They voice concerns because honesty is seen as a contribution, not a threat. They challenge ideas respectfully because the team believes that better solutions emerge when perspectives collide. In teams that resist change, the emotional climate is often shaped by silence, tension, or guarded professionalism. People do not feel free to express doubt and so doubt festers. Without emotional safety, adaptability becomes brittle.

Culture is almost always the deciding factor between teams that navigate change well and teams that do not. Two teams with identical resources, identical timelines, and identical training can produce completely different outcomes when one has built a culture of psychological safety and trust and the other has not. The change does not create that difference. It reveals it.

This is why culture is built in moments, not mandates. Not in strategy sessions or values workshops, but in the daily decisions made by everyone involved in a change about how to respond, what to acknowledge, and who to include.

A change leader who pauses before reacting when tension rises sets a tone. A change leader who listens without rushing to solve signals that people's experiences matter. A change leader who names what is true creates clarity. A change leader who invites people into the journey rather than directing them through it builds ownership. A change leader who models flexibility signals that adaptability is not just expected. It is safe. And it is not only the designated change leader who does this. Every person in the change, at every level, is either building that culture or quietly eroding it through the same daily choices.

These small consistent acts are the architecture of a change-ready culture. They do not require a program or a budget. They require intention, practised daily, in the smallest and most ordinary moments of leadership.

A change-ready culture is ultimately a culture full of change leaders. Not just the designated project lead or the appointed change manager, but people at every level who have developed the awareness, skills, and confidence to lead change from wherever they sit. One of the most important things this work has taught me is that change leadership is not the responsibility of a select few. It belongs to everyone. From frontline team members who spot early opportunities and champion new approaches in their daily work, to informal influencers who have built trust and credibility across the organization and can shape how people think about what is coming. From project and program managers rallying cross-functional teams, to HR and organizational development practitioners shaping the conditions for learning and adaptability. Every one of these people is a change leader, whether or not their title says so.

John C. Maxwell's framework on leadership levels describes the highest form of leadership as the leader who develops other leaders. At levels four and five, the leader's primary work is no longer managing tasks or even leading people through individual initiatives. It is building the capacity of the people around them to lead. In the context of change leadership, this principle is not aspirational. It is practical. The change leader who invests in developing the change capability of the people around them creates something more durable than any single initiative. They create an organization that does not need to wait for direction every time something shifts. Because the capacity to move with change has been built into the people themselves.

This is how a change-ready culture is built, one where agility is cultural rather than positional. When only the designated change leader is expected to navigate uncertainty, the organization is only as responsive as one person. When change leadership capability is distributed across teams and functions, the organization can move and adapt at every level simultaneously. That is the difference between an organization that manages change and one that leads it.

Building that kind of change-ready culture requires consistently attending to four things. **First, creating psychological safety** so people can speak honestly, take risks, and treat mistakes as learning rather than failure. **Second, ensuring leadership at every level visibly champions the change** and models the behaviours being asked of others. **Third, involving people from across the organization** in co-creating solutions, not just implementing them, because people support what they help to build. And **fourth, aligning the organization's systems, structures, and reward mechanisms** to reinforce the behaviours a change-ready culture requires. Change agility written in a values statement but punished in a performance review will never take root. Culture follows what the organization consistently rewards.

> Strategies evolve. Structures shift. Technologies are replaced. But culture endures. It carries people through changes that strategy alone could never sustain.

And organizations and leaders who invest in culture, not just in projects, who develop change capability in the people around them rather than simply directing change through them, create something that outlasts any single initiative. They create the capacity for their teams to face whatever comes next.

Over more than a decade of convening change leaders through The Change Leadership Conference and two decades of facilitating change leadership workshops with professionals and organizations across industries, sectors, and geographies, I have had the privilege of hearing from hundreds of practitioners and leaders about what they experiences in their work. These conversations have revealed remarkably consistent patterns across contexts and deserve to be named.

The first pattern is isolation. The most expressed experience among change leaders, regardless of seniority or sector, is the feeling of carrying the work alone. In workshops, when I ask people to describe the hardest part of leading change, the answer is rarely about methodology or process. It is about the weight.

They describe standing between strategy and delivery, holding the emotional load of the people around them while managing upward toward leaders who often do not fully understand the human complexity of what is unfolding. In Conference sessions year after year, I have watched rooms full of experienced professionals exhale visibly when someone else names this weight out loud, as if they had been waiting for permission to acknowledge it. This isolation is not a personal failing. It is a structural feature of how change leadership is positioned in most organizations.

The second pattern is identity tension. Change leaders consistently describe a tension between who the organization needs them to be and who they feel they need to be. They are expected to project confidence when they feel uncertain, to advocate for decisions they did not shape, and to support people through experiences they themselves are still processing.

The third pattern is the hunger for community. The leaders and practitioners I have spoken with, whether in a workshop of twelve people or a Conference room of several hundred, do not primarily seek more tools, more certifications, or more methodology. What they seek, overwhelmingly, is the experience of being in a room with people who understand the invisible weight of this work. People who do not need the role explained. People who have been in the difficult room and chosen to stay.

These patterns have shaped every chapter of this book. They are the reason the Soul exists as a dimension of the anatomy. They are the reason the book begins with the inner work before moving to the outer work. And they are the reason I believe that building a change-ready culture is not simply an organizational strategy. It is an act of care for the people who carry this work on behalf of everyone else. It is also why the work of building that culture cannot stop at the boundaries of a single team.

Building a change-ready culture within a single team is one challenge. Leading change across multiple teams, functions, and cultural contexts is another entirely. This is where some of the hardest work of change leadership takes place, in the spaces between teams, where misalignment, competing priorities, historical tensions, and genuinely different ways of seeing the world can quietly undermine even the most well-resourced initiative.

Organizations do not change in isolated pockets. They change through the collective movement of people who must work together even when their worlds, pressures, and perspectives differ.

You will recall from Chapter 1 the parable of the blind men and the elephant. Each person touching a different part and certain they understood the whole. Cross-functional and cross-cultural change works the same way. The IT leader is holding the tusk. Finance is holding the leg. HR is holding the ear. The frontline team is holding the tail. The head office is feeling one part. The call centre another. None of them are wrong. Every one of them is incomplete. The change leader's responsibility is not to tell each person what the elephant looks like. It is to create the conditions where everyone can finally see it together.

In organizations, different functions view the same change through genuinely different lenses. Technology teams think in systems, architecture, and timelines. HR teams think in capacity, behaviour, and impact on people. Finance teams think in budgets, constraints, and risk. Frontline teams think in workload, customer experience, and operational impact. None of these perspectives are wrong. They are simply incomplete. Change fails when these perspectives compete rather than complement.

Each team brings something valuable. Each sees something the others cannot. Change leaders who pull these perspectives together gain a fuller picture of the truth. Change leaders who allow them to remain disconnected find themselves managing a fragmented organization rather than leading a unified one.

Every organization contains a constellation of micro-cultures that operate by their own internal logic, often without anyone having consciously designed them. Head office communicates by direct email. People manage their own calendars and can engage with training on their own terms. But in a call centre, shifts are scheduled to the minute. Training cannot simply be sent to individuals. It moves through team leads, is built into shift patterns, and is delivered in ways that fit how that environment operates. The same change communicated the same way to both groups will land completely differently, not because either group is more resistant or less ready, but because their daily realities require different approaches.

When cross-functional alignment works, it looks like a rowing crew moving in perfect synchrony. Each person pulling at the same rhythm, in the same direction, with the same destination in mind. The boat does not just move. It glides. But when even one person is rowing differently, the whole vessel veers. The effort doubles. The direction becomes uncertain. Cross-functional change leadership is the work of getting everyone into that rhythm, not by demanding uniformity, but by creating enough shared understanding that people choose to pull together.

Think of a change leader operating across functions the way you think about a conductor leading an orchestra. Each section, strings, brass, woodwind, percussion, speaks a different musical language, has a different role, and produces a completely different sound. None of them can produce the full piece on their own. The conductor's job is not to play every instrument. It is to hold the full score in mind while ensuring each section understands its role in the whole, enters at the right moment, and listens as much as it plays. The most important skill is not technical mastery of any single instrument. It is the ability to create coherence from complexity.

Cross-functional change leadership works exactly this way. Change leaders do not need to be the expert in every function. They need to hold the full picture while helping each function understand how its contribution connects to the whole. And like a conductor, their greatest challenge is not the notes themselves. It is the timing, the listening, and the relentless work of ensuring that what sounds like complexity from inside any single function resolves into something coherent when seen from the full picture.

One of the most powerful abilities a change leader can develop in cross-functional environments is the ability to translate. Not to convert information from one format to another, but to convert meaning, to take the same truth and render it in the language the person receiving it is already listening in.

Change leaders who excel in cross-functional environments translate strategy into operational impact. They translate technical detail into human implications. They translate resistance into insight. They translate urgency into shared meaning. This translation is a form of respect. It tells people that their world has been understood well enough to speak to it honestly.

A finance leader needs the change translated into risk and return. A people leader needs it translated into what it means for the teams they are responsible for. A frontline team member needs it translated into what changes on Tuesday morning and who to call when something goes wrong. Same change. Different translations. All of them honest. All of them necessary. The language of change is nuanced and culture-specific, and a change leader knows when to adapt.

Early in my career, I had an experience that stopped me in my tracks and quietly changed how I lead. I had been working in the UK, where directness was simply the language of professional accountability. If a deliverable was outstanding, you named it. If a decision was pending, you said so. Not unkindly, but plainly. It was how work moved. Nobody took it personally because everybody understood it as the normal rhythm of getting things done. You could have a pointed exchange in a meeting and be sharing a drink with the same person an hour later. The work was the work. The relationship was the relationship. They existed in separate lanes.

When I moved to a new role in Canada, I brought that same directness with me. It felt like professionalism. It felt like accountability. In a steering committee meeting, I noted straightforwardly that we were waiting on sign-off from a senior leader. Nothing dramatic. Just a status update. The brass tacks. In the UK, it would have passed without a second thought. However, it did not pass without a second thought.

The feedback did not come to me directly or immediately. It came through my manager, carefully relayed, that the comment had not landed well. That naming the situation as I had named it had been experienced as a public calling out. That it had created discomfort at a level I had not anticipated and had not intended.

I remember sitting with that feedback and feeling genuinely surprised. Not defensive, though I will admit that impulse was there briefly. Mostly surprised. And then quietly unsettled in a way I had not expected. Because it made me question something I had always thought of as a strength. My directness and results-driven approach. It did not change who I was. But it changed how I paid attention to my environment.

I began to notice the cultural nuances. The way certain questions landed differently depending on who was in the room. The way the accountability language that felt neutral to me was being received and pointed out by others. The way the same words carried different weight depending on the invisible rules of the culture I was operating in. Rules that nobody had written down. Rules that nobody would explain to you until you had already broken one.

The lesson was not that one culture was wrong and another was right. The lesson was simpler and more demanding than that. As a change leader, it is not enough to know what you mean. It is your responsibility as the change leader to ensure the message is received as intended. And those two things are not always the same. This is what adaptive leadership looks like at the cultural level. Not abandoning your instincts but interrogating them. Asking whether the approach that has always worked for you is working here, in this room, with these people, inside this set of invisible rules.

Culture is not one layer. There are many operating simultaneously. Global culture. Organizational culture. Departmental micro-culture. Team culture. Each one shapes how people interpret messages, how they express agreement or resistance, how they relate to authority, and what they need from a change leader to move forward.

The change leader who reads only one layer and applies the same approach everywhere will keep encountering resistance that has nothing to do with the change itself. And the change leader who learns to read the varying layers, who develops the curiosity and humility to ask what is the invisible logic operating here before assuming the logic they already know, becomes something more than competent. They become genuinely adaptive.

Cross-functional trust grows through transparency, consistency, fairness, shared problem-solving, and the willingness to acknowledge each team's contributions with genuine specificity rather than generic appreciation. Trust is strengthened when change leaders ensure no one function dominates the conversation. When one team consistently feels unheard or undervalued, resentment grows, and alignment falters quietly, long before it becomes visible in any meeting or progress report.

Amy Edmondson's work on teaming and her research into how psychological safety operates in cross-functional and temporary team contexts found that the dynamics of trust and safety become more complex across team boundaries precisely because people have not built the relational history that makes trust easier. Cross-functional trust is not built solely through formal structures. It is built through the small consistent habits of organizations that have decided to lead change rather than simply manage it. In cross-functional change work, that history must be built deliberately and quickly.

Change leaders who understand this do not wait for trust to develop organically. They intentionally create the conditions for it through early conversations that acknowledge different realities, through decisions that visibly honour multiple perspectives, and through the consistent behaviour of someone who is genuinely trying to understand each world they work across.

When ownership becomes shared across functions, the change becomes a collective journey rather than a directive handed down from one part of the organization to another. People begin to support each other across boundaries. They fill gaps without being asked. They make decisions that consider the whole organization rather than only their department. Ownership turns collaboration into unity.

The true measure of cross-functional change leadership is not how teams collaborate during a single change. It is the culture of collaboration that exists before, during, and after. When collaboration becomes culture, agility becomes instinct. Change no longer feels like a disruption to be managed. It feels like a shared capability to be exercised. And change leaders who build that capacity, one relationship, one honest conversation, one well-translated message at a time, leave behind something that no project plan could ever deliver on its own.

A change-ready culture does not arrive fully formed. It is grown through the consistent choices made at every level of a change. Through the trust built across functions that did not previously speak the same language. Through the moments when a change leader paused to read the invisible logic of a room before assuming the logic they already knew. Through the conversations that named what was true, the translations that made the same message land differently for different people, and the daily acts of developing others into change leaders in their own right.

This is what it means to lead across teams, functions, and culture. Not managing the complexity from above. Moving through it together, with the curiosity to understand every layer and the humility to adapt at every turn.

Parts I and II of this book have explored who a change leader is and how they lead others through change. Part III turns to the world that change leaders are stepping into. A world moving faster, disrupted more frequently, and demanding a quality of change leadership that goes beyond what any single framework or methodology can provide. The chapters ahead are about applying everything you know, in a world that will test every part of it.

YOUR CHANGE LEADER JOURNAL

One Key Takeaway What insight about culture, cross-functional leadership, or collaboration resonated most deeply with me?

What Might Hold Me Back What assumptions about my own cultural or functional perspective might limit my ability to lead effectively across different teams or contexts?

The Action I Am Committed to Taking What one step can I take to develop the change leadership capability of someone around me, or to strengthen collaboration across a team or function I do not typically work closely with?

One Simple Step I Can Take Today I will reach out to someone in a different team or function and ask: "What does this change look like from where you sit?" Then listen without agenda.

PART III
APPLY

10

Leading Change in a Disruptive World

"The greatest danger in times of turbulence is not the turbulence. It is to act with yesterday's logic."
Peter Drucker

There is a realization that has quietly become a reality. Uncertainty is fast becoming the new certainty. The stability that was once the bedrock of how organizations planned, how institutions served, how communities organized, and how people understood their place within their work is no longer something we can rely upon. It is shifting beneath our feet in real time. And it is changing how we think, how we act, and how we lead change.

This is not a warning about the future. It is a description of the present. Stability was once the operating condition, and disruption was the interruption. Change management, as a discipline, was largely built on the same premise: that change was episodic, it had a beginning, a middle, and an end, and that the goal was to move people from one stable state to another as efficiently as possible.

That premise no longer holds. And the sooner change leaders fully accept this, the more equipped we will be to lead effectively in the world as it is.

Much of what we have inherited as change management methodology was designed for a world of episodic, bounded change. It assumes a stable starting state, a defined future state, and a managed transition between the two. It assumes that if the methodology is followed with sufficient discipline, the change will land as intended. It fundamentally assumes that change can be managed. This assumption is not only outdated. It is quietly doing damage.

When change leaders enter an organization carrying the implicit promise that change can be managed to a predictable outcome, they set an expectation that the reality of change will almost inevitably betray. People are told the transition will take eighteen months. It takes three years. People are told the disruption will be contained to one business unit. It ripples across four. People are promised that the methodology will guide them through. And when the methodology meets the complex, emotional, political, deeply human reality of how the change unfolds, the gap between promise and experience erodes the very trust on which the change depends.

The shift I am proposing is not the abandonment of structure. Structure matters. Planning matters. Rigour matters. But the orientation must change. From managing change to navigating it. From controlling outcomes to creating the conditions in which people can move through uncertainty with confidence, agency, and support. From the illusion of predictability to the practice of presence.

This is not a semantic distinction. It changes what change leaders prioritize, how they measure success, and what they promise the people around them. A change leader who promises to manage the change to a defined outcome has set themselves up to fail in a complex environment. A change leader who promises to navigate the change with honesty, adaptability, and genuine care for the people going through it has set themselves up to lead. That is the shift this book is built on.

We are not moving through a period of disruption that will eventually return to predictability. We are living in an era where disruption has become the atmosphere itself. The question is no longer how to manage change. It is how to lead change when it is continuous, when the environment is rewriting its own rules faster than any planning cycle can track, and when the people looking to change leaders for steadiness are themselves navigating more uncertainty than any previous generation has experienced in peacetime.

To lead change in a disruptive world, a change leader must first see the world clearly. Not as they wish it were, not through the lens of how things used to work, but as it is. And what it is right now is a convergence of forces that are reshaping organizations, institutions, communities, and the very nature of how we work and serve simultaneously. Artificial intelligence is no longer a future consideration. It has arrived, and with each passing year, it reaches further into the nature of work itself, reshaping what organizations and institutions need, what skills remain essential, and what it means to contribute. The specifics will continue to evolve in ways no one can fully predict.

What will not change is the leadership challenge at the centre of it: when the tools and conditions of work shift faster than people can adapt, the people themselves need something steady to hold onto. Those who navigate technological disruption well are rarely the ones with the deepest technical understanding. They are the ones who understand that behind every system, every upgrade, and every restructured role is a human being asking whether they still matter, whether their contribution is still valued, and whether there is still a place for them in what is being built. That question does not age. And it will not. What technology has set in motion will not slow down or wait. It will continue to be one of the most powerful forces reshaping how organizations operate, how public services are delivered, and how people work within them. Change leaders who are not intentional about how they engage with this reality will find that the distance between where they are and where the world is moving grows harder to close with each passing moment.

Economic uncertainty has shifted from a cyclical to a structural concern. The volatility in markets, supply chains, public budgets, and institutions is no longer driven solely by predictable patterns. It is increasingly shaped by forces that intersect and amplify one another: geopolitical decisions, trade realignments, technological disruption, and the breakdown of assumptions about cooperation and stability that once provided a degree of predictability for those leading change across every sector. Decision-makers who once planned five years ahead are navigating a world where conditions can shift significantly within a single planning cycle, whether they lead a corporation, a government ministry, a nonprofit, or a community organization.

Geopolitical shifts are reshaping the context within which the world operates in ways that would have been difficult to imagine a decade ago. The architecture of the international order, the rules, institutions, and agreements that governed global trade, security, and cooperation for much of the past eighty years, is under visible strain. Change leaders are navigating through a world in which underlying assumptions can shift dramatically based on decisions made far beyond their sphere of influence.

The workforce itself is transforming. People bring different expectations to work than they did ten years ago. The relationship between an organization and its people, built on assumptions of loyalty, tenure, and long-term employment, is being renegotiated in real time. Hybrid work has permanently altered not just where people work, but how they experience belonging, how teams build trust, and how change leaders create connection across distributed environments. The social contract of work is changing, and leaders who are still managing to the old contract will find themselves losing the people they most need.

These forces at one time used to arrive separately. Now they arrive together, amplifying one another, creating a complexity that resists simple analysis and defies easy solutions. This is the environment in which today's change leaders are being asked to lead. Not a complicated environment, where more analysis eventually yields the right answer, but a complex one, where answers emerge only through navigation, not planning.

In January 2026, Canadian Prime Minister Mark Carney stood before the World Economic Forum in Davos and delivered what many described as one of the most significant speeches heard at that gathering in recent memory. He was not speaking as a change leader in an organizational sense. He was speaking as a change leader on the global stage, as head of government, about the shifting world order. But what he described, and how he described it, captures something that every change leader operating in this era needs to hear.

Carney named the moment for what it was. "We are in the midst of a rupture, not a transition," he said. He described the fading of the rules-based international order not as a gradual evolution but as a fundamental break, a shift so significant that the frameworks, institutions, and assumptions built over decades could no longer be relied upon in the way they once were. And then he said something that carries weight for anyone leading change: "The old order is not coming back. We should not mourn it. Nostalgia is not a strategy. But from the fracture, we can build something better, stronger, and more just." He was not simply dismissing what had been. He was naming the moment with honesty and then turning toward what was possible. This is precisely what change leadership requires.

The reason this speech matters for change leaders is not political. It matters because Carney was modelling on a global stage exactly what this chapter is about. He was naming reality as it is, not as he might have preferred it to be. He was publicly acknowledging that a model that had delivered real value for decades was no longer adequate for the world as it had become. He was releasing an old framework not with celebration but with honesty, then turning toward what was possible in the new reality.

This is the work of change leadership. Not just at the geopolitical level, but at the organizational, community, institutional, and personal level. The rupture Carney described on the world stage has its equivalent in every context where change is being led: the moment when a change leader must acknowledge that the old playbook is no longer adequate, and that nostalgia for it, however understandable, is not a strategy.

> One of the most disorienting aspects of leading in a disruptive world is that there is no longer a fixed playbook to follow.

This is not a complaint. It is a description. And understanding it changes how a change leader approaches their role. For most of the modern management era, leadership had a discernible playbook. The approaches that worked in one context could be adapted and applied in another. Experience accumulated into expertise, and expertise provided the foundation for confident decision-making. Organizations, governments, and community institutions invested heavily in developing this expertise, capturing best practices, building playbooks, and training leaders to apply proven approaches to new situations. This was rational. It worked, for a long time, in a world where conditions were sufficiently stable that experience remained relevant.

That world is gone. Not because experience has stopped mattering, but because the rate at which the conditions that generated best practices are changing now outpaces the rate at which those practices can be reliably applied. The playbook is not just changing. It is being rewritten continuously, often while change leaders are still using it. A communication approach that worked brilliantly during one change initiative may fall flat in the next because the emotional landscape of the workforce has shifted. A stakeholder engagement strategy built on the assumption of stable organizational hierarchies may be undermined by structural changes that have realigned power and influence. A change methodology developed for a world of sequential, bounded projects may be inadequate in an environment of continuous, overlapping change.

This does not mean everything that worked before is useless. Principles of leadership remain. The fundamentals of change leadership, building trust, creating psychological safety, communicating with honesty and humanity, listening deeply, maintaining purpose under pressure, these are not going to be superseded. They are, if anything, more important in a disruptive world than they were in a stable one. But the specific applications, the tactical choices, the sequencing, the emphasis, must be generated freshly in response to each context rather than pulled from a pre-existing model and applied wholesale.

The shift this requires of a change leader is significant. It requires moving from the comfort of applying what you know to the discipline of reading what you are currently facing. From executing a proven approach to developing the capacity to create one. From expertise as the answer, to curiosity as the foundation.

There is a sentence widely attributed to the futurist Alvin Toffler that becomes truer with each passing year: the illiterate of the 21st century will not be those who cannot read and write, but those who cannot learn, unlearn, and relearn. Most of us are extraordinarily good at learning. We have built careers and reputations on the capacity to acquire knowledge, develop expertise, and apply what we know. But learning is only one-third of what the disruptive world now requires. The harder work, and the work most of us have not yet been fully invited to do, is the unlearning.

Unlearning is not forgetting. It is not the erasure of experience or the dismissal of everything that came before. It is the deliberate examination of an assumption, a model, or an approach that has been carried forward, and the honest asking of whether it still serves the world you are actually in. It requires something that expertise tends to work against: the willingness to become a beginner again in at least some dimension of your leadership identity and practice, to hold what you know lightly enough that new understanding can enter.

This is genuinely difficult. Not because people are stubborn or resistant, but because professional identity is so often built on the certainty of what one knows.

Someone who has spent twenty years developing deep expertise is not simply carrying knowledge. They are carrying a way of seeing: a set of assumptions about how people behave, how change works, what leadership requires, what good looks like, what is possible and what is not. Those assumptions were formed through real experience. Many of them remain entirely valid. But some are holding change leaders back, not because they were ever wrong, but because the conditions that made them right have changed.

The challenge is that from the inside, a constraint built from experience feels indistinguishable from wisdom. Both feel like knowing. The leader who insists on face-to-face communication as the only real form of connection is drawing on real experience. The leader who believes that resistance is a problem to overcome rather than information to understand learned that from somewhere too. The leader who equates speed of delivery with quality of leadership built that belief through years of reward and recognition. These are not failures of thinking. They are the natural accumulation of experience in a world that has since shifted.

Unlearning asks us to do something rare and difficult: to examine the assumptions that feel most certain, most familiar, most like bedrock, and to ask honestly whether they are still serving the work.

The three-part movement that Toffler described, *learn, unlearn, relearn,* is not a linear sequence. It is an ongoing practice, a posture that change leaders must adopt and maintain, particularly in periods of significant disruption. **Learn:** stay curious, stay open, keep acquiring what is genuinely new. **Unlearn:** examine regularly what is being held onto that no longer serves. **Relearn:** be willing to build a fresh understanding of existing paradigms from what the current reality is showing you, rather than from what a previous reality once confirmed.

This practice is not comfortable. It runs against the grain of how expertise works and how leadership confidence is typically constructed. But in a world of continuous disruption, it is one of the most important capacities a change leader can develop. History is generous with examples of what happens when organizations and leaders choose the comfort of the old model over the confrontation of a new reality.

Blockbuster did not fail because it lacked talent or resources. At the peak of its success, it operated thousands of locations across multiple countries and held a brand that millions of customers recognized and trusted. When

Netflix approached Blockbuster's leadership in its earliest days with an acquisition offer, they declined. The logic of the existing model was too strong. Physical retail had worked, reliably and profitably, for decades. The idea that a DVD-by-mail service could challenge that dominance was easy to dismiss, and dismissing it felt like prudent management rather than dangerous complacency. What Blockbuster's leadership could not see was that the certainty they felt about their model was itself the risk. They were not defending a strategy. They were defending an assumption about how entertainment would always be consumed. By the time the evidence was undeniable, the argument was over.

The story of Blockbuster is more complex than any single narrative captures. Debt from a leveraged buyout played as significant a role as strategic blindness, but the core pattern holds: when certainty in a working model becomes indistinguishable from complacency, the model is already in danger.

Kodak's story is, if anything, more instructive. Kodak engineers invented the digital camera. The technology was developed inside the company, by people who understood photography better than almost anyone in the world. Leadership set it aside because it threatened the film business that was generating the returns shareholders expected. The failure was not one of innovation. It was one of unlearning. Kodak could not release the model that had made it great, even when it held in its own hands the evidence that the model was ending. This was not a failure of intelligence. Kodak's leadership understood exactly what digital photography would do to their film revenues. It was a failure of the will to let go. A distinction worth naming, because it is the same failure that presents itself, at smaller scale, in every change initiative where a working model stands in the way of a necessary one. The technology existed. The will to let go of what it would displace did not.

IBM demonstrates that a different outcome is possible, even when the challenge is enormous. By the early 1990s, IBM was in genuine crisis. The company that had helped define the personal computing era was losing ground at a speed that seemed, to many observers, to signal an irreversible decline. Revenue was falling sharply. The business press was openly questioning whether IBM had a viable future. The organization that had seemed unassailable was facing something more destabilizing than competition. It was facing the obsolescence of its own identity. Everything IBM had been built on, its dominance in hardware, its culture of formal hierarchy, its model of long-term client relationships anchored to physical products, was being challenged by a world moving toward software, services, and speed.

What happened next was not simply a strategic pivot. It was an organizational act of unlearning at scale. Lou Gerstner arrived as CEO in 1993 without a technology background, which was considered, at the time, either remarkably bold or desperately reckless. What Gerstner brought was something IBM's own leadership had struggled to access: the capacity to see the organization without the assumptions that had accumulated through decades of success. He did not look at IBM and see what it had always been. He looked at it and asked what it could become given the world as it had already become.

Gerstner resisted the prevailing wisdom that IBM should be broken into smaller units. Instead, he identified something IBM's own people had been undervaluing: the company's ability to integrate complex solutions across platforms for large enterprise clients. In a world growing more interconnected and more technologically complex, that capacity was increasingly rare and increasingly valuable. But recognizing it required letting go of the identity that had defined IBM for decades, and rebuilding around a fundamentally different understanding of where IBM's real strength lay.

The transformation was neither quick nor painless. It required releasing roles, restructuring businesses, and asking people at every level of the organization to examine and release assumptions about what IBM was and what it stood for. But what IBM demonstrated was that unlearning at an organizational scale is possible when leaders are willing to face reality directly and release the models that once generated success but no longer serve the world as it has become.

The through-line connecting these three stories is not strategy. It is the presence or absence of the willingness to unlearn. Blockbuster and Kodak clung to models that their own evidence was already challenging. IBM found the courage to let go and build again. The same pattern plays out beyond the corporate world. Public institutions that have resisted redesigning services around how people live today. Community organizations still running on models built for a different generation's needs. The details differ. The dynamic is the same.

Byron Katie, whose work on examining the stories we hold about reality has influenced leaders and coaches around the world, offers a deceptively simple observation: when you argue with reality, you lose. Not sometimes. One hundred percent of the time. In change leadership, this is not philosophical. It is practical. The leaders and organizations that struggle most in disruptive environments are not those that lack intelligence or resources. They are the ones still arguing with a reality that has already moved on, still insisting that the conditions they prepared for are the ones they are facing, still waiting for the disruption to pass so they can return to the world they knew.

My response to this, and what I try to bring to every engagement is: rather than arguing with reality, begin by seeing it. Not as you would like it to be. Not through the filter of how things used to work. But as it is. This is harder than it sounds because the desire to return to familiar ground is genuinely strong, particularly for those who built their confidence on the reliability of that ground. But reality is not the enemy of good leadership. It is the foundation of it. Everything begins with the willingness to see clearly.

None of this takes place in a vacuum. Change leaders are not navigating disruption alone. They are navigating it while holding responsibility for the people around them, who are also experiencing the uncertainty, who are also being asked to release familiar models, and who are also unsure whether their skills and contributions will remain relevant in the emerging world.

The emotional stakes of this are significant. Research in neuroscience suggests that ambiguity activates threat-related circuits in the brain, producing responses similar in effect to those triggered by physical danger. Areas of the brain associated with threat detection do not distinguish reliably between an approaching predator and an uncertain future. When the environment feels unpredictable, the nervous system responds with heightened vigilance, narrowed creative capacity, and a powerful impulse toward familiar patterns. This is not a weakness. It is human biology. But it means that those who want their people to remain open, curious, and adaptive in a disruptive environment must first address the emotional experience of uncertainty rather than simply the operational demands of change.

People do not need those leading them to have all the answers. They need them to be present with the uncertainty rather than pretending it does not exist. They need honesty about what is known, transparency about what is not, and steadiness that signals the uncertainty can be navigated even when it cannot be resolved. They need change leaders who will model the very unlearning and relearning being asked of the team: who will say, I held this assumption, I have examined it, and I am willing to let it go. Who demonstrate through their own behaviour that releasing what no longer serves is an act of leadership, not a failure of competence.

We have explored resilience as the roots that hold in a storm, the capacity to recover, refocus, and re-engage when a hard moment passes. That dimension of resilience remains true and essential. But a disruptive world asks for something more, and something different. Not because the roots no longer matter, but because the storm is no longer an event. It has become the climate.

Resilience, in a disruptive world, asks to be understood differently than before. When disruption is continuous, when the ground keeps shifting, and there is no stable state to recover toward, resilience can no longer be measured by how well you bounce back. It must be understood as a state of being.

It is not the capacity to endure, which implies pushing through something toward a point of relief. It is not the capacity to recover, which implies returning to something familiar. It is the capacity to keep evolving, to grow differently in response to whatever the moment requires, without losing the essential truth of who you are as a change leader.

This kind of resilience does not announce itself. It is visible in the change leader who examines an assumption they have held for years and releases it without shame. In the change leader who encounters an unfamiliar challenge and meets it with curiosity rather than defensiveness. In the change leader who has been depleted by the pace of change and chooses, deliberately and without apology, to restore themselves so they can show up fully for the people depending on them. It is not a single act. It is a practice. A posture. A way of moving through a world that will not stop changing by choosing, every day, to keep growing within it.

Resilience, understood this way, is less something you call upon and more something you embody. It is built quietly, in the daily choices to stay curious, to examine rather than defend, to remain present rather than retreat. And it is what allows change leaders to lead with integrity and humanity, not just through one hard season, but across an entire career spent navigating a world in motion.

There is a particular kind of courage that a disruptive world asks of change leaders, and it is quieter and more demanding than the courage of bold decisions or public commitments. It is the courage to look clearly at what is true, even when the truth is uncomfortable. The courage to release an assumption or method that has provided confidence and identity, without knowing exactly what will replace it. The courage to say, in front of the people you lead, that you do not have the answer yet, but that you are willing to navigate toward it together. The courage to be wrong about something you were once certain about, and to let that wrongness be visible rather than defended.

This kind of courage is contagious. When change leaders embody it, the people around them feel safer being honest about their own uncertainties, outdated assumptions, and fears about the changing landscape. They feel less alone in the experience of not knowing. And when people feel less alone in not knowing, they become more capable of the learning, unlearning, and relearning that the disruptive world is asking of all of them.

When I reflect on the changes I have witnessed in this era, what stands out most is not the scale of the disruption itself. It is the quality of those navigating it. The people who struggled were rarely lacking in intelligence or capability. They were holding too tightly to certainty: the conviction that their experience had already equipped them fully for what was coming, that what had worked before would work again if applied with enough discipline. Disruption does not respond to discipline applied to the wrong model. It responds to the willingness to examine the model, release what no longer serves, and rebuild from what the current reality is showing.

Those who thrive stay curious. They ask hard questions of their own assumptions. They create environments where unlearning is understood as a form of strength rather than a confession of inadequacy. And they understand that in a world where the playbook is being rewritten in real time, the most valuable thing they can offer is not certainty, but the demonstrated capacity to move honestly and humanely through the absence of it.

> The world is changing. So must the people who navigate it. By pausing to reflect deeply on what still serves and what no longer does, by being willing to face reality directly, releasing what has been outgrown, and remaining genuinely open to what the moment is making possible.

This is the work of change leadership in a disruptive world. It begins not with a new framework or a better strategy, but with the courage to see clearly, the humility to release what no longer serves, and the willingness to lead others into a future that is constantly taking shape.
There is a particular kind of freedom that comes when a change leader stops arguing with the reality in front of them and starts working with it instead. The ground may

not be as solid as it once felt. The map may no longer match the terrain. But those who are willing to look clearly, release what no longer serves, and stay genuinely curious about what is still possible are the ones the people around them will choose to follow into the uncertain and necessary future ahead.

Navigating disruption requires more than courage and clarity. It requires an evolving set of capabilities and capacities built for the world as it now is. In the next chapter, we turn to the skills that will define change leadership in the years ahead, not the skills that once served a more predictable world, but the ones the future is actively asking for.

YOUR CHANGE LEADER JOURNAL

One Key Takeaway What did I read here that I already know to be true but have been unwilling to fully face?

What Might Hold Me Back Which assumption, model, or approach am I still holding onto that may no longer serve the world I am leading in?

The Action I Am Committed to Taking What is one thing I am willing to unlearn right now, and what might become possible on the other side of it?

One Simple Step I Can Take Today I will ask someone I trust: "Is there something I believe or practice that you think no longer serves us?" Then listen without defending.

11

Future-Ready Change Leader

"The measure of intelligence is the ability to change."

Albert Einstein

We previously explored a world that is constantly evolving, one that change leaders must be continuously adept at navigating. A world shaped by disruption, accelerating technology, geopolitical uncertainty, and the collapse of assumptions that once felt permanent. The previous chapter asked whether you were willing to see reality clearly and lead within it. The question here is different.

In a world that is constantly evolving, what type of change leader are you becoming. Not what tools do you need. Not what methodologies will serve you.

But what capabilities, what ways of thinking and feeling and showing up, will distinguish the change leaders who thrive from those who find themselves perpetually overwhelmed by a world that keeps moving faster than their frameworks and old thinking can accommodate.

Several capabilities are emerging as essential to how future-ready change leaders think, feel, and show up. Among the most important are **learning agility, sensemaking, emotional mastery, empathy, storytelling, and systems thinking.** And beneath all of them, the one that holds everything together: courageous decision-making in the absence of clarity. These are not items on a competency framework. They are not credentials to be earned or boxes to be checked. They are ways of being that develop over time, through practice, reflection, and the willingness to stay honest about where you are still growing.

Think of water as it moves through a river's varied terrain. It does not choose a technique for each rock or bend it encounters. It simply keeps moving, finding depth in the channels it returns to most often, adapting its shape to what it meets, and becoming more fluid the further it travels. These capabilities work in the same way. They do not operate independently. They build on each other, deepen through each other, and together form the inner architecture of a change leader who is genuinely ready for what the future requires.

The World Economic Forum has been tracking the evolution of leadership and workforce skills for over a decade through its Future of Jobs research. Their findings consistently point in one direction. Technical skills rise and fall with each wave of technology. Human, relational, and cognitive skills continue to grow in importance. Analytical thinking, creative problem solving, empathy, adaptability, and emotional intelligence consistently appear at the top of every future skills projection. Several surveys indicate that more than half the capabilities considered essential today did not appear on comparable lists a decade ago.

This tells us something important. The future will not primarily distinguish change leaders by what they know. It will distinguish them by how they think, feel, adapt, connect, and respond when the situation offers no clear answer. By their ability to navigate ambiguity and lead others through it.

There is a line widely cited in leadership circles, often attributed to Darwin, that survival belongs not to the strongest or most intelligent but to those most adaptable to change. This principle has never been more applicable. In a world where change arrives faster than strategy can accommodate, adaptation is no longer a desirable leadership trait. It is a foundational one. It asks change leaders to approach the future with openness rather than fear, curiosity rather than defensiveness, and the willingness to release what no longer serves before the ground shifts beneath them.

A large part of being adaptable is **learning agility,** the ability to learn, unlearn, and relearn in continuous cycles. Research from the Center for Creative Leadership and the work of organizational psychologist Warner Burke on learning agility consistently shows that this capability is one of the strongest predictors of leadership effectiveness in complex and changing environments. And yet it is among the most difficult to cultivate, not because it requires exceptional intelligence, but because it requires a particular kind of courage. The courage to release what you have spent years mastering.

Those who struggle most in rapidly changing environments are not those who lack intelligence or experience. They are those who have so thoroughly identified with their expertise that releasing any part of it feels like a personal diminishment. Their knowledge has become their identity, and so new knowledge feels like a threat rather than an addition.

I encountered this during a change program I was leading. One of the senior managers had built an exceptional reputation over nearly two decades. They were widely regarded as the foremost expert on the way things worked in that organization, the person others came to when nothing made sense. In many ways, they were the institutional memory of the entire division. But the change being implemented would make much of that institutional knowledge obsolete. New systems, new processes, new ways of structuring the work entirely. And this manager, for all their brilliance and genuine commitment to the organization, could not move. Not because they opposed the change, but because their identity was tied to the very thing they were being asked to let go of.

In a quiet moment after one of the sessions, they said something I have thought about many times since. "I have spent twenty years becoming the person everyone comes to. I have no idea how to be the person who does not know."

That sentence names something people feel but rarely say out loud. The deepest resistance to learning agility is not intellectual. It is existential. It is the fear that letting go of expertise means letting go of identity. The work of building a future-ready change leader often begins there, in that quiet, uncomfortable space between who you have been and who the future is asking you to become.

> Future-ready change leaders carry their expertise lightly. They treat what they know as a foundation to build from, not a fortress to defend.

Satya Nadella captured this precisely when he described the cultural shift he brought to Microsoft: from a know-it-all organization to a learn-it-all organization. That shift did not occur in the company's technical architecture. It happened in the identity of its people. Under his leadership, Microsoft regained its relevance and became one of the most studied examples of organizational renewal in the modern era. What changed was not what people knew. It was how they related to not knowing.

Learning agility opens into something equally essential: **sensemaking.** As the world becomes more interconnected, the situations change leaders face increasingly resist straightforward answers. While there are patterns and principles to draw from, there is rarely a correct answer to be found simply by analysing long enough. There is instead a need to sit in ambiguity long enough to understand what is happening before deciding how to respond. Sensemaking is the ability to do exactly that. It sits between observation and action, between receiving information and knowing what to do with it. It is the ability to observe patterns in uncertainty, to listen for what is not being said, to hold competing interpretations simultaneously without forcing premature closure, and to create shared meaning from conditions that feel chaotic to those navigating them.

Change leaders who develop sensemaking capability do not eliminate the uncertainty their teams feel. They make it bearable. They help people understand what is happening, why it matters, and what can be influenced, even when the path ahead is still forming. They help others navigate change not by having all the answers but by helping make sense of the questions. In an environment where people are frequently disoriented, they look to their change leaders not for certainty but for coherence. A change leader who can say, here is what we know, here is what we do not know, and here is how we will navigate the uncertainty together, is offering something more valuable than any roadmap. They are offering a way of making sense of the change. Yet none of this is possible if a change leader cannot first manage their own internal landscape.

Emotional mastery is one of the most critical future capabilities and one of the most consistently underestimated in leadership development. It is not about suppressing emotion or performance of composure. It is about understanding the relationship between your internal state and your external impact. Psychologist Elaine Hatfield's research on emotional contagion, developed further in the leadership context by Daniel Goleman, confirms what most people already sense from their own experience of being in a room with someone who is calm, and someone who is not. People catch the emotional tone of those around them, particularly those they look to for direction and safety.

When a change leader is overwhelmed, teams absorb that overwhelm. When a change leader is grounded, teams find their own footing.

This means that how a change leader manages their own emotional responses is not a private matter. It is a leadership decision with organizational consequences. The capacity to pause before reacting, to breathe into discomfort rather than escape it, to acknowledge emotion without being governed by it, these are not soft practices. They are intentional and strategic. In hybrid and distributed environments, where presence is mediated through screens and tone must carry across digital distance, emotional mastery becomes even more essential. People are reading the change leader's emotional signal through compressed bandwidth. What comes through is not the full complexity of the leader's inner state. It is a simplified version that the team then amplifies.

As explored in The Heart Chapter, one of the most important things emotional mastery has taught me is what becomes possible the moment you stop reacting and start listening. That shift, small as it sounds, changes not just a single conversation but the entire nature of a relationship. The stakeholder who erupts in a meeting is rarely angry about the thing they appear angry about. Emotional mastery is the capability that allows a change leader to know that, and to respond to what is real beneath what is visible. It is the difference between a change leader who manages the surface and a change leader who reaches the source.

The future will reward change leaders who invest in developing what might be called emotional range: the ability to hold more emotional complexity without defaulting to either numbness or reactivity. This includes the capacity to acknowledge fear without feeding it, to hold uncertainty without projecting false certainty, and to stay curious and present in conversations that push against personal limits.

Closely related to emotional mastery, and perhaps the most paradoxical capability of the future, is **empathy.**

The paradox arises because artificial intelligence is rapidly developing the ability to simulate what was once the exclusive domain of human connection. AI can now analyze tone, recognize emotional cues, generate responses calibrated to sentiment, and adapt communication style in real time. In some interactions, AI-generated responses appear more patient, more consistent, and more attuned to language than human responses shaped by stress, distraction, or bias. Coaching platforms, mental health tools, and leadership development applications are already leveraging these capabilities at scale.

This raises a question the next generation of change leaders must grapple with honestly. If AI can replicate the surface expressions of empathy, what becomes of the change leader who relies on technique without depth? Who uses the language of listening without genuinely listening? Who performs psychological safety without creating it?

When my mother had to navigate several significant decisions in choosing between specialists or services, the pattern I noticed was striking. Her decisions were rarely driven by credentials or technical reputation alone. She consistently chose the specialist who made her feel seen, heard, and genuinely cared for. In a world where technology increasingly outpaces human capability in diagnostic accuracy and information processing, what moved her was the one thing technology cannot replicate: the presence of a human being who genuinely cared about her experience. That is not sentiment. It is a signal about where human value will increasingly reside as AI capability grows. The same dynamic plays out every day.

People do not simply need information or even technically excellent guidance. They need to feel that the person leading them genuinely cares whether they are okay.

The rise of AI makes human empathy more essential, not less. What AI cannot replicate is the lived experience of genuinely caring about another person's reality. AI can mirror warmth, but it does not feel it. It can reflect language that appears compassionate, but it does not carry the weight of shared humanity that makes compassion meaningful in moments of real difficulty. When a team member receives difficult news about a role change, when a long-tenured person faces the loss of a familiar way of working, when a group of anxious people need someone to stand with them in the uncertainty, they are not looking for a sophisticated emotional response.

They are looking for a human being who is genuinely present with them.

Change leaders who cultivate genuine empathy, not as a technique but as a way of paying sustained attention to the people they lead, will be irreplaceable in ways that no technological capability can displace. The more environments become mediated by tools and screens, the more people will orient themselves around the humans who make them feel truly seen. In a world increasingly shaped by artificial intelligence, the most powerful thing a change leader can offer is something no system can generate: their full, undivided human presence.

Storytelling is another capability the future-ready change leader will increasingly need, and it is consistently underinvested in. Change leaders can easily categorize storytelling as a communication style, an optional aesthetic choice rather than a fundamental leadership function. But in an environment of constant disruption, where people are being asked to release familiar structures and move toward futures they cannot yet fully see, story is not decoration. It is the primary mechanism through which human beings make meaning. If The Heart chapter explored the emotional intelligence that connects change leaders to people, storytelling is how that connection carries meaning across distance, across teams, across an entire organization or community. It is empathy given language.

Facts inform. Stories move. Data creates the intellectual case for a change. Story creates the emotional permission to make it. A change leader who can translate the complexity of a change, whether in an organization, a community, or any group navigating uncertainty, into a narrative that people can see themselves inside, that connects where things have come from to where they are heading and why the journey matters, is doing something that no amount of well-designed communication templates can accomplish. They are helping people understand their place in something larger than themselves.

This is particularly relevant to data. Numbers are among the most underutilized storytelling tools available to change leaders, not because data lacks power, but because change leaders routinely present data as evidence rather than as narrative. The same statistic lands completely differently depending on whether it is offered as a percentage on a slide or translated into human terms. The difference between saying "seventy percent of our people report uncertainty about their roles" and "seven out of every ten people you work with walked into this building today without knowing what their job will look like next month" is the difference between information and urgency. One invites analysis. The other invites action. The skill is not in the data itself. It is in the translation of data into the human reality it represents, and in knowing your audience well enough to adapt how that story is told.

Systems thinking connects all these capabilities together. Peter Senge, whose foundational work in *The Fifth Discipline* shaped how organizations understand complexity, argued that the ability to see wholes rather than parts, and to understand how individual decisions ripple across interconnected systems, is one of the most important and most underdeveloped principles in organizational life. That argument is even more relevant today than when he first made it.

Change leaders who think in straight lines miss the full picture. A decision that appears straightforward in one part of an organization ripples across teams, functions, relationships, and cultures in ways that are rarely fully anticipated. Systems thinking asks change leaders to look for those ripples before they create their own dynamics. It asks them to hold in mind not only what a change is designed to do, but what it will touch, what it will disrupt, and who will bear costs that do not appear in the project plan.

Organizations, communities, and teams are living systems, not machines. They have their own patterns of self-protection, their own informal logics that shape how people behave, regardless of how a process is designed. Change leaders who adopt a systems perspective develop the patience to work with the system rather than simply pushing harder against it.

Underlying all these capabilities is the one that brings them together and perhaps demands the most: courageous decision-making in the absence of clarity.

This is not the courage of dramatic moments or public declarations. It is the quieter, more sustained courage of making consequential decisions with incomplete information, communicating those decisions honestly without pretending certainty exists, and adjusting course when new information demands it without treating the adjustment as a failure. In stable environments, good decision-making was largely a matter of gathering enough information and applying the right analysis. In environments like the one we now inhabit, that model breaks down. The information is always incomplete. The analysis is always partial. The cost of waiting for certainty before deciding is often higher than the cost of deciding imperfectly and adjusting.

What future-ready change leaders need is what might be called principled uncertainty: the capacity to make decisions grounded in values and purpose even when outcomes are unclear, to communicate with transparency about what is known and what is not, and to model through every iteration and every adjustment that changing course is not evidence of poor leadership but evidence of honest and adaptive leadership. This is the capability that holds everything else together, because *learning agility, sensemaking, emotional mastery, empathy, storytelling, and systems thinking* all require the courage to act without a guarantee. Without that courage, every other capability remains theoretical.

When I reflect on the change leaders I have encountered throughout my career who have navigated the most difficult and uncertain conditions with integrity, they share certain qualities. They are curious rather than defensive. They are comfortable not knowing and genuinely interested in discovering. They hold their expertise as a gift to offer rather than a position to protect. They remain, regardless of how much they have achieved, fundamentally oriented toward learning. And they understand at a deep level that the most important thing they bring to any room is not what they know, but who they are and who they are willing to become.

The capabilities explored in this chapter develop over time, through each difficult conversation, each moment of genuine listening, each decision made with integrity in conditions of uncertainty. They deepen not through training alone but through practice and reflection and the willingness to stay honest about where you are still growing.

The change leaders who will shape the future are not those who have mastered these capabilities. They are those who are genuinely committed to developing them, one encounter at a time. And that commitment begins not with a program or a plan, but with a question.

Not what do I need to know to lead change in the world ahead. But what posture do I need to take.

The world does not need change leaders who have all the answers. It needs change leaders who have the courage to keep asking better questions, the humility to learn from what those questions reveal, and the humanity to bring others with them through the uncertainty of not yet knowing. That is not a gap in change leadership capability. It is its highest expression.

YOUR CHANGE LEADER JOURNAL

One Key Takeaway Which future-ready capability resonated most strongly with where I am in my leadership right now, and why?

What Might Hold Me Back What habit, attachment, or belief might make it most difficult for me to develop this capability?

The Action I Am Committed to Taking What is one intentional step I can take to strengthen a human-centered leadership capability?

One Simple Step I Can Take Today I will ask someone whose judgment I trust: what quality do you think I could develop further as a change leader?

12

The Change Leader

"The privilege of a lifetime is to become who you truly are."

Joseph Campbell

There are moments in a change leader's journey when the work stops feeling like something you are doing and begins to feel like something you are. The frameworks you once reached for consciously have become instinct. The questions you once rehearsed before difficult conversations now arrive without preparation. The steadiness you once performed in high-stakes moments is no longer performance at all. It is simply who you are in the room.

These moments of recognition are quiet. They rarely announce themselves. You are in the middle of a conversation, or standing at the front of a room, or sitting across from someone whose fear is visible but unspoken, and something in you responds in a way that the person you were five years ago could not have. That is the moment of recognition. Not an arrival. A confirmation.

This chapter is not a summary of what you have learned. It is an acknowledgment of who you are as a change leader. And there is a significant difference.

Being a change leader is like stepping into a river that has been flowing long before you arrived. You step into the water and feel its movement around you. You sense its direction, even if you cannot see beyond the next bend. You notice that the water continually flows. It never stops. It adapts to rocks, curves, and shifting terrain with a kind of quiet intelligence. It does not resist what it encounters. It moves with it, reshaping its path and renewing its momentum as it goes. It learns the landscape by travelling through it.

This is how a change leader evolves. Not in a classroom or a workshop or even in a book. In the current. In the actual experience of standing in uncertain terrain with people who are looking to you for steadiness, and choosing, again and again, to stay present rather than retreat. The river does not fear the next bend. It trusts its own movement. And when you lead through times of genuine difficulty and uncertainty, you too are shaped, softened, strengthened, and expanded by the journey itself.

You have reached this point having explored the anatomy of a change leader. Not as a framework to be memorized but as an identity to be inhabited. The Head, the Heart, the Hands, and the Soul are not four separate concepts. They are four dimensions of a single way of leading, and they work in concert in every meaningful moment of change leadership.

The Head gave you clarity. Not certainty, which no change leader can offer, but the grounded thinking that helps others find their footing in conditions of genuine confusion. **The Heart gave you connection.** The understanding that people do not follow strategies; they follow the humans behind them, and that being truly present with someone in their uncertainty is one of the most powerful acts of leadership available to you. The **Hands gave you the courage to act**, to move before the path is fully visible, to make progress visible to the people around you, even when the finish line is not. And the Soul gave you the foundation beneath all of it, the clarity of purpose that keeps you grounded when everything around you is moving, the values that hold when easier choices present themselves, the resilience that recovers without losing direction.

> Together, these four dimensions do not make you a perfect change leader. They make you a present one. And in change leadership, presence is worth more than perfection.

The Change Leadership Conference was never something I planned for or even knew to name. It found me. Slowly, and then all at once.

For many years, it felt like a purpose. It felt like passion. I could see the impact of failed change, the cost to people, to organizations, to communities, and I knew that what I was doing mattered. But for a long time, it felt more like a calling I was answering than an impact I could see. You do the work because you believe in it and that it is making the desired impact.

Then the stories began to arrive. The first one, I was not expecting. The day after our very first Conference, my phone rang. The person calling had not been there. They had not registered, had not sat in any of the sessions, had not been in the room for any of it. But their colleagues had. And what those colleagues had come back and said was not that the programme had been well run, or that the content had been useful, or that they had picked up some practical tools. What they had said was that they had found their tribe.

I sat with that for a long time. The word tribe. Not content. Not value. Tribe. Belonging. It named something I had not yet known how to name myself. The work was not simply filling a gap in the market for change leadership development. It was creating a place where people who had spent years feeling slightly outside the mainstream of their profession could finally feel that they belonged to something. That someone had built a room specifically for them.

The stories kept arriving in different forms. A practitioner stopped me at a different event some months later. They were emotional before they had finished their first sentence. What they described was not a particular session or speaker or moment in the programme. They described what it had felt like to be in the room. To look around and see people who carried the same invisible weight they had been carrying alone for years. They used the word representation. They used the word seen. And then, quietly, they said that something had shifted in how they showed up in their own work since. That they had walked back into difficult situations with a confidence they had not brought with them before.

Those encounters did not stop. Emails that arrived weeks or months after a Conference. People who stopped to speak to me at other events. Each one arrived quietly. And each one carried more weight than I can easily describe. During the years of the COVID pandemic and beyond, I asked myself more than once whether we could continue. Whether The Change Leadership Conference could survive what the world was asking of all of us. Those questions were real, and they were not easy. But as we reached ten years, and as this book moved from something I was writing toward something that would exist in the world beyond me, something became clear. Change leadership did not simply find me. It chose me. And whatever the current brings, however the water flows, I will adapt. Not with resistance, but with the same qualities this book asks of every change leader: moving forward, evolving, learning, unlearning, and relearning, travelling through this lifetime with the privilege of being exactly who I was born to be.

That is the work. That is the invitation. You are the change leader who can answer it. Not to become something new. To be, more fully, what you already are.

As change leaders, there will be moments where the path seems unclear. Situations where the stakes feel high and the answers feel distant. Moments when people look to you for reassurance, direction, or hope and you are not sure you have what they need. In those moments, return to your anatomy. Let your Head bring clarity. Let your Heart bring compassion. Let your Hands bring action. Let your Soul remind you who you are.

This is not a formula. It is a practice. And practice does not produce perfection. It produces depth. The change leader who has practiced leading with the Head and the Heart and the Hands and the Soul for years moves differently through difficult moments than they did when they began, not because they have removed the difficulty, but because they have developed a relationship with it. They know how to be in it without being undone by it.

You may not always feel ready. That is not a sign that you are not. Readiness as a change leader is not the absence of doubt. It is the presence of commitment. The willingness to step into the current, even when the current is fast, even when you cannot see around the bend, even when the water is cold. The river does not wait until conditions are ideal. It flows.

Change leadership is not something you do on certain days when the stakes are high. It is something you carry into every conversation, every decision, and every relationship. It is the way you listen when someone is struggling to say what they mean. The way you hold steady when a room fills with anxiety. The way you stay curious when you would rather be certain. The way you choose people over process when the two come into conflict. It is a practice of being. Not arrival. Not completion. Being.

The world will continue to change in ways none of us can fully predict. Technologies will evolve. Organizations will restructure. The geopolitical landscape will shift in ways that challenge every assumption. Familiar structures will give way to emerging ones. And in every one of these moments, there will be people who need someone to help them make sense of what is happening, to walk with them through the uncertainty, to believe in their capacity when they have temporarily stopped believing in it themselves. That is the work. That is the invitation. You are the change leader who can answer that invitation.

I want to leave you with something personal. I have spent my career in rooms where change was happening to people who needed someone to stand with them in it. Over time, I have come to understand the change leader role as something closer to a sherpa than a guide. A sherpa does not carry you to the summit. They walk beside you, knowing the terrain, reading the conditions, and trusting that you have what it takes to make the climb yourself.

I have seen change leaders choose courage when compliance would have been easier. I have watched people discover reserves of resilience they did not know they carried. I have been in moments where one conversation shifted everything, not because of a framework, but because of genuine human presence. And I have learned, again and again, that the capacity for that kind of presence is not reserved for a few exceptional people. It is available to anyone willing to do the inner work.

That is what this book has been about. Not techniques. Not methodology. The inner work of being a change leader who can show up fully for the people navigating the most difficult moments of their professional and organizational lives.

You have already done that work. You have been doing it. And it matters, more than you may fully understand right now.

When you bring genuine presence into a conversation, someone feels less alone in their uncertainty. When you choose clarity over comfort, someone else finds the courage to be honest. When you stay in the difficulty rather than manage it from a distance, someone discovers they can stay in it too.

This is how change spreads. Not through mandates or announcements. Through the quiet, cumulative effect of one human being choosing to lead with intention in the presence of another.

There is a particular quality to the change leader who has done the inner work. It is not certainty. It is not the absence of doubt. It is a kind of quiet groundedness that others feel before they can name it. A willingness to be fully present in the most difficult rooms. An ability to hold steady not because nothing is moving, but because they know what is anchoring them. That is what these chapters have been building toward. Not a credential. A way of being. The river keeps moving. So do you.

I believe in the kind of change leader you are. Not because the path has been easy or the answers have always been clear. But because you showed up anyway. And the world is different because of it.

Your future is not a place you arrive at. It is a place you create. Go forward and create it with courage, with integrity, with all four dimensions of your anatomy working together in service of the people who need you to be exactly who you are.

The Change Leader.

YOUR CHANGE LEADER JOURNAL

One Final Reflection

Who am I as a change leader? What do I stand for, how do I choose to show up, and what kind of change leader am I committed to being from this point forward?

Epilogue

Hello, Change Leader

Every day, people walk into rooms carrying more than anyone can see.

They carry the weight of decisions that were made without them and changes they did not choose. They carry quiet fears about whether they are capable enough, visible enough, valued enough. They carry the memory of past change that went badly and left a mark. They carry the person they are at home, the worries they tucked away before the meeting started, the grief or the joy or the exhaustion they brought through the door and set politely to one side. They carry all of this behind a professional composure that the world largely accepts at face value.

Behind every title is a human being. Behind every confident presentation is someone who rehearsed it and was still not sure. Behind every person who pushed back loudly in a meeting is someone trying to protect something that matters to them deeply. Behind every change leader who held the room together is someone who went home that evening and finally let themselves feel the weight of it.

This is the world you lead in.

Change leadership does not stay inside the walls of the organizations where it happens. It travels. When a person feels genuinely seen and supported through a difficult change at work, they go home differently. When people discover that they can trust their change leader, that trust does not evaporate when they leave the building. It becomes part of how they understand what leadership can be, and part of the standard they will bring to every room they ever lead in the future.

You may never see most of this. The ripple effects of human-centred change leadership are largely invisible to the person creating them. A conversation that shifted someone's entire relationship to their own courage. A moment of acknowledgment that helped someone believe in their capacity again. A decision to slow down and listen when it would have been easier to push forward. These things travel further than you know, and they last longer than any project plan.

I have always believed that a rising tide lifts all boats. Change leadership is not about standing at the front. It is about lifting the water level for everyone around you. When you lead with integrity, you give the people watching permission to believe that kind of leadership is possible. When you choose humanity over expediency, you make the culture around you a little more human. And those small choices accumulate into something real.

We do not know what the future holds. We never have. What we do have is today. This awareness. The decision you make in the next room you walk into is about who you will be and how you will show up.

Hello, Change Leader.

I see you. I honour the work you do, the courage it requires, and the humanity you bring to it.

The world needs you. Not a polished version of you. Not a certain version. The real version. The one who leads with presence, who listens beneath the surface, who stays in the difficulty because you know that is where people need you most.

A rising tide lifts all boats. May you be part of the tide.

About the Author

Yvonne Ruke Akpoveta MBA, C.Dir. is a Change Management Strategist and Advisor, a change leadership advocate, and the founder of The Change Leadership, a global community dedicated to preparing professionals, change leaders, and organizations to successfully lead and navigate change in today's fast-paced and disruptive environment.

With over 20 years of experience, Yvonne has worked with a broad range of organizations globally to lead and manage strategic, technology, and regulatory change initiatives. Her clients have included RBC, TD, Deloitte, Loblaws, the Ontario Public Service, and JP Morgan Chase. Her work is known for being practical as it is deeply human, grounded in the belief that when change is done right, it yields invaluable benefits to stakeholders and the wider community.

She serves on numerous boards with a focus on serving humanity and dismantling inequity. Her proprietary Change Leadership DNA framework, Discover, Navigate, Apply, has guided practitioners and senior leaders through some of the most complex change initiatives of the past decade.

Yvonne holds a BSc Honours in Business Information Technology and Marketing from London Guildhall University, an MBA from Warwick Business School, a Change Leadership Certificate from Cornell University, and a Chartered Director designation from DeGroote and McMaster University.

The Anatomy of a Change Leader is her fourth book. Her first, The Change You Want! Change Your Mindset, and Change Your Life, was published in 2014. Through publications, thought leadership, and ongoing contributions, she has become a trusted voice for practical and human-centred approaches to leading and navigating change in a rapidly evolving world.

www.thechangeleadership.com | www.yvonnerukeakpoveta.com

Notes and References

Chapter 1 - The Head

1. **Hesburgh, Theodore M.** Confirmed attribution. "The very essence of leadership is that you have to have vision. You can't blow an uncertain trumpet."
2. **Neuroscience of uncertainty.** Text uses qualified language ("research suggests"). See: Rock, D. (2009). Your Brain at Work. Harper Business.
3. **VUCA framework.** Originated with the U.S. Army War College, late 1980s. See: Johansen, B. (2009). Leaders Make the Future. Berrett-Koehler.
4. **Communication repetition.** Practitioner principle in change communication and adult learning. Not a specific research finding.
5. **Nadella, Satya.** See: Nadella, S. (2017). Hit Refresh. Harper Business.

Chapter 2 - The Heart

6. **Angelou, Maya.** Widely attributed. Earliest verified source: Carl W. Buehner, in Evans, R. (1971). Richard Evans' Quote Book. No primary Angelou source established. Carried as attributed.
7. **"People don't care how much you know."** Widely circulated saying. Not attributed in the text. Not connected to Theodore Roosevelt.

8. **Mirror neurons.** Text uses qualified language ("some researchers propose"). The link between mirror neurons and human empathy is scientifically contested. See: Rizzolatti, G. and Craighero, L. (2004). The Mirror-Neuron System. Annual Review of Neuroscience, 27, 169-192.
9. **Edmondson, Amy C.** See: Edmondson, A. (1999). Psychological Safety and Learning Behavior in Work Teams. Administrative Science Quarterly, 44(2), 350-383. Edmondson, A. (2018). The Fearless Organization. Wiley.
10. **Brown, Brene.** See: Brown, B. (2012). Daring Greatly. Penguin/Avery. Brown, B. (2018). Dare to Lead. Random House.
11. **Goleman, Daniel.** Cognitive vs. compassionate empathy. See: Goleman, D. (1995). Emotional Intelligence. Bantam Books. Goleman, D., Boyatzis, R., and McKee, A. (2002). Primal Leadership. Harvard Business Review Press.
12. **Empathy and team performance.** The claim that leaders who demonstrate empathy build higher-performing teams draws on: Goleman, D. (2002). Primal Leadership (see note 12). Center for Creative Leadership. (2023). Empathy in the Workplace: A Tool for Effective Leadership. ccl.org.
13. **Change curve.** See: Kübler-Ross, E. (1969). On Death and Dying. Macmillan. Bridges, W. (1991). Managing Transitions. Perseus Books.

Chapter 3 - The Hands

14. **Martin Luther King Jr.** Attribution uncertain. No verified primary King text found. Fuller version: "Take the first step in faith. You don't have to see the whole staircase, just take the first step."
15. **Edison, Thomas.** Widely attributed. No verified primary source established.
16. **Amabile, Teresa and Kramer, Steven.** See: Amabile, T. and Kramer, S. (2011). The Progress Principle. Harvard Business Review Press. Note: the dopamine claim draws on separate neuroscience research, not Amabile and Kramer's behavioral methodology.
17. **Dopamine and progress.** See: Rock, D. (2009). Your Brain at Work. Harper Business.
18. **Roosevelt, Franklin D.** 30 fireside chats across 12 years. See: Miller Center, University of Virginia. millercenter.org.

Chapter 4 - The Soul

19. **Nietzsche, Friedrich.** Paraphrase of sentiment in Nietzsche's Twilight of the Idols (1889). Popularized by Frankl, V. (1946). Man's Search for Meaning. Beacon Press.
20. **Burns, Ursula.** See: Burns, U. (2021). Where You Are Is Not Who You Are. Amistad.

21. **Polman, Paul.** See: Polman, P. and Winston, A. (2021). Net Positive. Harvard Business Review Press.

Chapter 5 - The Human Side of Change

22. **Senge, Peter M.** Widely attributed. No verified primary source confirmed. Carried as attributed.
23. **Change curve.** See note 14.
24. **Brain threat response.** The claim that the brain's threat response activates when familiar structures shift draws on the same body of research cited in Chapter 6 (Rock, SCARF model, note 31) and Chapter 7 (LeDoux, note 37). See those notes for full citations.
25. **Mulally, Alan.** See: Hoffman, B.G. (2012). American Icon: Alan Mulally and the Fight to Save Ford Motor Company. Crown Business.
26. **Google Project Aristotle.** Google's Project Aristotle and Amy Edmondson's academic research (1999) are two distinct but complementary bodies of work that independently identified psychological safety as the primary differentiator of high-performing teams. See: Google re:Work. (2016). rework.withgoogle.com. See also note 10.

Chapter 6 - Influence, Adaptive Leadership, and Navigating Hidden Dynamics

27. **Iacocca, Lee.** Iacocca, L. and Novak, W. (1984). Iacocca: An Autobiography. Bantam Books. The quote appears in Chapter 1. Page number varies by edition; verify against the specific printing before publication.
28. **Edelman Trust Barometer.** Edelman. (2024). 2024 Edelman Trust Barometer. edelman.com/trust/2024/trust-barometer. The finding that people place greater trust in someone like themselves than in senior executives is a consistent finding across multiple years of this research.
29. **Heifetz, Ronald.** See: Heifetz, R. (1994). Leadership Without Easy Answers. Belknap Press. Heifetz, R. and Linsky, M. (2002). Leadership on the Line. Harvard Business Review Press. Heifetz, R., Grashow, A., and Linsky, M. (2009). The Practice of Adaptive Leadership. Harvard Business Review Press.
30. **Rock, David.** SCARF model: Status, Certainty, Autonomy, Relatedness, Fairness. See: Rock, D. (2008). SCARF: A Brain-Based Model for Collaborating with and Influencing Others. NeuroLeadership Journal, 1, 1-9.
31. **WIIFM principle.** Established practitioner principle in motivation psychology and adult learning.
32. **"People support what they help to create."** Rooted in Lewin, K. (1947). Frontiers in Group Dynamics. Human Relations, 1(1), 5-41.

33. **Maxwell, John C.** See: Maxwell, J.C. (1998). The 21 Irrefutable Laws of Leadership. Thomas Nelson. Law 1: "Leadership is influence — nothing more, nothing less."

Chapter 7 - Communication That Moves the Needle

34. **Shaw, George Bernard.** Widely attributed. No verified primary source in Shaw's published works established. Carried as attributed.
35. **Ardern, Jacinda.** Facebook Live address, March 23, 2020. See: New Zealand Royal Commission COVID-19 Lessons Learned (2024).
36. **Emotional processing.** See: LeDoux, J. (1996). The Emotional Brain. Simon & Schuster.
37. **Zenger and Folkman.** See: Zenger, J. and Folkman, J. (2016). What Great Listeners Actually Do. Harvard Business Review, July 14, 2016.
38. **Maxwell, John C.** Good Leaders Ask Great Questions. Center Street, 2014.

Chapter 8 - Leading and Sustaining Momentum Through the Middle

39. **Confucius.** Widely attributed. Attribution disputed. Carried as attributed.
40. **Shackleton, Ernest.** All 28 men survived. See: Shackleton, E. (1919). South. William Heinemann.

Lansing, A. (1959). Endurance: Shackleton's Incredible Voyage. Carroll & Graf.

41. **Amabile and Kramer.** See note 17.
42. **Seligman, Martin E.P.** Resilience as a cultivated trait. See: Seligman, M. (2011). Flourish. Free Press.
43. **Change fatigue.** The observation that change fatigue is a significant contributor to change initiative outcomes is documented in change management practitioner research. See: Prosci. (2023). Best Practices in Change Management. 12th ed. prosci.com.

Chapter 9 - Leading Across Teams, Functions, and Culture

44. **"If you want to go fast, go alone."** Traditional African proverb. No single attributable source.
45. **Schein, Edgar H.** Culture as accumulated shared learning. See: Schein, E. (2017). Organizational Culture and Leadership. 5th ed. Jossey-Bass.
46. **Google Project Aristotle.** See note 27.
47. **Nadella, Satya.** See: Nadella, S. (2017). Hit Refresh. Harper Business.
48. **Edmondson, Amy C.** Teaming and psychological safety in cross-functional contexts. See: Edmondson, A. (2012). Teaming: How Organizations Learn, Innovate, and Compete in the Knowledge Economy. Jossey-Bass.
49. **Blind Men and the Elephant.** Ancient parable with roots in Jain, Buddhist, and Hindu traditions. Approximately 2,400 to 2,500 years old.

50. **Maxwell, John C.** Leadership levels framework. See: Maxwell, J.C. (2011). The 5 Levels of Leadership: Proven Steps to Maximize Your Potential. Center Street.

Chapter 10 - Leading Change in a Disruptive World

51. **Drucker, Peter F.** Widely attributed. Well documented across Drucker's published work.
52. **Carney, Mark.** Address to the World Economic Forum Annual Meeting, Davos, January 20, 2026. Verify final wording against official transcript at pm.gc.ca. Confirm title held at time of publication.
53. **Toffler, Alvin.** The "learn, unlearn, relearn" version in circulation is attributed to Herbert Gerjuoy, not Toffler. Toffler's actual quote from Future Shock (Random House, 1970, p.414) differs. Carried as "widely attributed to Toffler."
54. **Katie, Byron.** See: Katie, B. and Mitchell, S. (2002). Loving What Is: Four Questions That Can Change Your Life. Harmony Books.
55. **Blockbuster.** See: Keating, G. (2012). Netflixed: The Epic Battle for America's Eyeballs. Portfolio/Penguin. Note: Blockbuster's failure involved both strategic decisions and significant debt from a leveraged buyout; the manuscript acknowledges this complexity.
56. **Kodak.** Kodak engineer Steve Sasson invented the digital camera in 1975. Leadership chose not to

commercialize it to protect film revenues. See: Lucas, H. (2012). The Search for Survival. Praeger.

57. **IBM and Gerstner.** See: Gerstner, L. (2002). Who Says Elephants Can't Dance? Inside IBM's Historic Turnaround. Harper Business.
58. **Neuroscience of ambiguity.** The claim that ambiguity activates threat-related circuits in the brain draws on: Rock, D. (2008). SCARF (see note 31). LeDoux, J. (1996). The Emotional Brain (see note 37). Note: the text uses "threat-related circuits" in recognition that responses to psychological ambiguity and physical threat, while overlapping, are not neurologically identical.

Chapter 11 - Future-Ready Change Leader

59. **Einstein, Albert.** Widely attributed. No verified primary source established. Carried as attributed.
60. **World Economic Forum.** World Economic Forum. (2025). Future of Jobs Report 2025. January 2025. Available at: weforum.org/publications/the-future-of-jobs-report-2025/. Key findings: 39% of key skills are expected to change by 2030; 63% of employers cite the skills gap as the primary barrier to business transformation; technological skills, particularly AI and big data, are projected to see the most rapid growth alongside human skills such as resilience, creative thinking, and adaptability.

61. **Darwin attribution.** Definitively not a Darwin quote. Originates with Megginson, L.C. (1963). Lessons from Europe for American Business. Southwestern Social Science Quarterly, 44(1), 3-13, p.4. Darwin never wrote or said this. The manuscript correctly carries this as widely cited in leadership circles rather than a confirmed Darwin quote.
62. **Learning agility.** See: De Meuse, K.P., Dai, G., and Hallenbeck, G.S. (2010). Learning Agility: A Construct Whose Time Has Come. Consulting Psychology Journal: Practice and Research, 62(2), 119-130. Burke, W.W. (2017). Organization Change: Theory and Practice. 5th ed. SAGE.
63. **Emotional contagion.** See: Hatfield, E., Cacioppo, J., and Rapson, R. (1993). Emotional Contagion. Cambridge University Press. Goleman, D., Boyatzis, R., and McKee, A. (2002). Primal Leadership. Harvard Business Review Press.
64. **Senge, Peter M.** See: Senge, P.M. (2006). The Fifth Discipline: The Art and Practice of the Learning Organization. Rev. ed. Doubleday.
65. **Skills evolution.** The claim that the capabilities considered essential for leadership today look significantly different from those valued a decade ago is consistent with WEF Future of Jobs reporting across multiple editions (see note 61). The 2025 edition reports that 39% of key skills are expected to change by 2030.

Verify the exact phrasing in the manuscript against the WEF 2025 data before publication.

Chapter 12 - The Change Leader

66. **Campbell, Joseph.** See: Osbon, D.K. (Ed.). (1991). A Joseph Campbell Companion: Reflections on the Art of Living. HarperCollins, p.9. Confirmed attribution. Note: a variant of this quote — "The privilege of a lifetime is to become who you truly are" — is widely attributed to Carl Jung online, but no verified primary source in Jung's published works has been established. The Campbell attribution is confirmed with a specific verified source and is used here.

Further Reading

The following books have informed the thinking in this work and are recommended for readers who wish to go deeper on the themes explored across these chapters.

Amabile, Teresa, and Steven Kramer. The Progress Principle: Using Small Wins to Ignite Joy, Engagement, and Creativity at Work. Harvard Business Review Press, 2011.

Brown, Brene. Daring Greatly: How the Courage to Be Vulnerable Transforms the Way We Live, Love, Parent, and Lead. Gotham Books, 2012.

Brown, Brene. Dare to Lead: Brave Work, Tough Conversations, Whole Hearts. Random House, 2018.

Burke, W. Warner. Organization Change: Theory and Practice. 5th ed. SAGE Publications, 2017.

Campbell, Joseph. A Joseph Campbell Companion: Reflections on the Art of Living. Edited by Diane K. Osbon. HarperCollins, 1991.

Edmondson, Amy C. The Fearless Organization: Creating Psychological Safety in the Workplace for Learning, Innovation, and Growth. Wiley, 2018.

Edmondson, Amy C. Teaming: How Organizations Learn, Innovate, and Compete in the Knowledge Economy. Jossey-Bass, 2012.

Frankl, Viktor E. Man's Search for Meaning. Beacon Press, 1959.

Gerstner, Louis V., Jr. Who Says Elephants Can't Dance? Inside IBM's Historic Turnaround. Harper Business, 2002.

Goleman, Daniel. Emotional Intelligence: Why It Can Matter More Than IQ. Bantam Books, 1995.

Goleman, Daniel, Richard Boyatzis, and Annie McKee. Primal Leadership: Unleashing the Power of Emotional Intelligence. Harvard Business Review Press, 2002.

Heifetz, Ronald A. Leadership Without Easy Answers. Belknap Press, 1994.

Heifetz, Ronald A., Alexander Grashow, and Marty Linsky. The Practice of Adaptive Leadership: Tools and Tactics for Changing Your Organization and the World. Harvard Business Press, 2009.

Katie, Byron, and Stephen Mitchell. Loving What Is: Four Questions That Can Change Your Life. Harmony Books, 2002.

Lansing, Alfred. Endurance: Shackleton's Incredible Voyage. Carroll & Graf, 1959.

Maxwell, John C. The 21 Irrefutable Laws of Leadership. Thomas Nelson, 1998.

Maxwell, John C. The 5 Levels of Leadership: Proven Steps to Maximize Your Potential. Center Street, 2011.

Maxwell, John C. Good Leaders Ask Great Questions. Center Street, 2014.

Nadella, Satya. Hit Refresh: The Quest to Rediscover Microsoft's Soul and Imagine a Better Future for Everyone. Harper Business, 2017.

Polman, Paul, and Andrew Winston. Net Positive: How Courageous Companies Thrive by Giving More Than They Take. Harvard Business Review Press, 2021.

Rock, David. Your Brain at Work: Strategies for Overcoming Distraction, Regaining Focus, and Working Smarter All Day Long. Harper Business, 2009.

Schein, Edgar H. Organizational Culture and Leadership. 5th ed. Jossey-Bass, 2017.

Seligman, Martin E.P. Flourish: A Visionary New Understanding of Happiness and Well-being. Free Press, 2011.

Senge, Peter M. The Fifth Discipline: The Art and Practice of the Learning Organization. Rev. ed. Doubleday, 2006.

World Economic Forum. Future of Jobs Report 2025. World Economic Forum, January 2025. weforum.org/publications/the-future-of-jobs-report-2025

www.ingramcontent.com/pod-product-compliance
Lightning Source LLC
LaVergne TN
LVHW091044080826
845145LV00002B/621